BLACK'S ULTIMATE GUIDES

Native American Herbalist's Bible

Your 7-Part Guide
to Natural, Traditional
Remedies for
Modern Ailments

ISBN 978-1-7393830-5-3

About the author

Jacob Black is a relatively young herbalist who grew up witnessing how others used medicinal plants to successfully treat different illnesses. Having learned from herbal practitioners for over 25 years, particularly his Cherokee grandmother, he knows how to use herbal medicines effectively for himself and his family. In this book, Jacob focuses in detail on the 101 herbs that he believes are the most useful and effective.

Aside from the natural healing properties of herbs, he sees using herbal remedies as a sustainable and cost-effective way of maintaining a healthy mind and body. He and his young family have been enjoying the health benefits of plants for many years. That positive experience has encouraged him to educate others as well and help them achieve a healthy life through natural ways, and so this book was written.

While he believes that western medicine has its own place for curing diseases, he still prefers herbal treatments for modern ailments and other illnesses as much as possible.

When not working, you can find Jacob gardening, reading botany books, and teaching his own children the ways of the Creator.

DEDICATED TO
SHIRLEY, TINA, AND CONNIE:
SEED, SOIL, AND GARDENER.

THIS BOOK EXPLAINS THE SPIRITUAL BELIEFS BEHIND NATIVE AMERICAN HEALING PRACTICES AND WHY YOU, THE READER, SHOULD CONSIDER USING NATURAL PRODUCTS OVER SYNTHETIC DRUGS PRESCRIBED BY TODAY'S DOCTORS FOR MODERN AILMENTS. THE BOOK PROVIDES A COMPREHENSIVE LIST OF 101 MEDICINAL PLANTS TOGETHER WITH THE SPECIFIC ILLNESSES THEY CAN HELP HEAL AND STATES WHICH PARTS TO USE, HOW TO CONSUME, AND WHEN TO AVOID.

Contents

PART ONE

JACOB'S STORY

Jacob's Story

"Over 200 drugs that have been or still are listed in the Pharmacopeia of the United States or the National Formulary were first used by American Indians, but neither reference acknowledges this fact. Thus, the tremendous benefits we've derived from indigenous knowledge of native plant medicines go largely uncredited."

M. KAT ANDERSON USDA NRCS

Picture this scene: we are in a dappled, green forest, and the weather is kind. It is early morning, the perfect time to harness the power of the rising sun in the herbs we need. Searching for a specific leaf shape and color, the memory map we hold in our hearts directs us slightly to the left, close to that branch, and then curves around the back of that trunk, close to the stream. We remember the flower blooming here in May and the scent that permeated then, but maybe today, we are looking for the root or berry. A shaft of sunlight reminds us that we must send our thanks for this moment, surrounded by abundant foliage, before any herb is picked. We gently pluck enough to thank the plant which gives us fruit, pleading for healing to occur, and thanking the plant for its gift to us. The herb must never be cleared out entirely. We only select healthy berries, perhaps some leaves, but the plant remains intact. Sometimes we offer a gift or smoke a pipe to express our thanks. We carefully collect leaves, flowers, berries, stems, roots, and sometimes bark, celebrating the gladness that fills our baskets and hearts. Our herb collection brings with it a heightened awareness of the seasons. They represent the cyclical nature of leaves budding in spring, growing in abundance in summer, and then falling to earth to mix into the soil throughout fall and winter. Next year's growth depends on the earthworms feeding on the leaves and enriching the soil.

Such is the life of Jacob Black, the author of this book, a collector of Native American herbs. This book offers alternatives for dealing with illness through conventional medicine, the accepted part of modern life. Yes, a trip to your doctor often results in an excellent diagnosis, a listening ear, good advice about lifestyle changes, and a prescription for pharmaceutical drugs. However, our trip to the field, lake, mountain, or forest is a spiritual experience and substantiates the Native American approach to health and well-being. This book explores illness as a physical symptom and the body's response to grief, stress, or bereavement, modern work patterns like night shifts, and even emotional disagreements with the damage done to our natural environment by our consumer-led lifestyles. Here in the forest, the wind moves leaves that rustle in a wave on the canopy, our eyes are filled with color, and our ears slowly attune to bird song, animal life, and bees collecting nectar. These ideal conditions may seem dreamlike, but these are the methods followed by indigenous people for thousands of years before the onset of "civilization."

Eastern approaches, such as acupuncture for pain relief and the consumption of certain plants to boost health, concur with Native Americans. They believe that illness is probably lodged in the physical body as some aspect of imbalance that needs adjustment before we regain our health. This book presents a holistic approach. You can start healing your body, mind, and spirit using herbs found in local places or homegrown in your backyard and experimenting with Native American methods to boost vitality, ease pain, and improve your overall well-being.

The making of the healer

For many "medicine men" and shamanic transformations, an accident or near-death experience is the nudge to re-evaluate the life you have chosen and helps you to become the more rounded individual life has planned for you. Jacob Black's career began as an agricultural ranch hand clearing debris from riding trails, harvesting firewood, and doing odd jobs.

"At first, I only did what I was asked, plowing fields, planting seed, spraying pesticides on crops without much protection. Cutting trees and slicing years of growth into timber gave me a great knowledge of the grain of the wood, the drying times required, and sometimes the surprise fungi that would pop up. It had not even occurred to me that I was destroying habitats for wildlife daily, and the harmful pesticides we used freely in those environments began to take their toll on me and my body." Jacob hardly recalls the huge, falling tree that trapped his body underneath it for hours to become the wounded Guardian of the Land. Other ranch workers struggled to free him while he slipped in and out of consciousness. There is no memory of the emergency helicopter landing at the local hospital. Still, Jacob remembers a prolonged rehabilitation period where he could not walk properly, and he stumbled through hospital corridors for many dark months.

Jacob recalls the nightmares he believes were partly due to the medicine supplied to ease his inflammation and pain, which did not deal with his long-term unease about modern agriculture. Visits by his grandparents brought back childhood holidays spent in the forests with them, collecting. His grandmother reminded him of his secret childhood friend, Tiyohali, who led him to discover the black cohosh she needed for her arthritis. She told him this meant lizard in Cherokee, but it could also mean snake or reptile. She had taught him about only collecting in the morning and how he could only remove tiny amounts of bark "from the east side" of the tree.

As he lay insomniac on his hospital bed, searching back through childhood, he suddenly found the prayer she had taught him to chant for the bark, the root, and the leaf offered in the early morning light. Hospital libraries were full of books, but he only craved the knowledge stored in his grandmother's mind, and she spent hours discussing her recipes and methods while he lay on his back with his leg in traction. Perhaps the combination of medicine and her wish to re-trace her collecting sites was the final push he needed to complete the painful physiotherapy stretches, pining for the fresh air and his woods.

The idea that somebody "owns" land is alien to Native Americans, who were offered money for ownership of their land by settlers. The Native American lifestyle involved seasonal traveling, foraging, and collecting, which could not be limited by a piece of paper claiming "ownership." The land is not owned by any one of us; Jacob maintains, "the land owns us," and we transit our particular landscape as long as we breathe. The landscape is an integral and essential element of the veneration of Native American tribes throughout the Americas. High mountains were close to the sun and moon, recognizing these celestial bodies' significant effects on our days and nights, our seasons, and the cyclical ability to live off the land. Caves were linked to the darkness, rest, dream time, and the place where the ancestors retreated after death. Certain animals, such as bears and eagles, are also recognized as spirit animals and deities. They are called upon to perform ceremonies, provide food, and guide humankind so that life is an interdependent cycle of living, a life in harmony with nature itself. Whether Native Americans were farmers or hunters, nature was revered as the provider of life itself, and nothing was wasted. A tenet of the relationship was that one never picked to destroy any plant, only carefully and precisely removing what was needed.

Animals, birds, and aquatic life were co-owners of the land, in a shared partnership of plants, trees, and all animals, birds, insects, and marine life that inhabit the earth, holding their unique place in the order of the planet. Anybody who has stared upwards at the orangy-pink glow of a rising sun and felt glad to be alive understands this message: "If you protect me, I will provide you with abundance." *Black's Ultimate Native American Herbalist's Bible* shares that this earth was gifted to us by the Creator and must be protected by us. Herbs to improve our health will flourish, ensuring humanity respects our natural environment and its inhabitants. All of his beliefs are Jacob Black's Native American philosophy in a nutshell. Any love we pour into our planet repays us with beauty, food, water, shelter, and herbs to soothe our aches and pains.

What this book offers

If you are a beginner at collecting or growing herbs, then start from here and immerse yourself in the history of Native American herbal practices, the methods used, and an introduction to herbalism in PART 2.

If you use modern medicine when you need to but are keen to learn more about the impact these herbs can have on general well-being, PART 3 will examine why you should consider herbal remedies. You can absorb the experience as if you are one of the Guardians of the Land, which the ancestors tell us all humanity used to be.

If you already have some knowledge of herbs, PART 4 shares eleven of the most commonly used Native American herbs with some recipes to get you started.

Perhaps you need an accurate description of a particular Native American herb? Then go immediately to PART 5, which has all-inclusive information, including pictures, to identify an individual herb, which ailment it helps, and how to use it.

Or maybe you have a particular ailment that requires an immediate herbal remedy? Then head to PART 6, where you will find an a-z of conditions and potential herbal solutions.

Unsure of the details surrounding particular herbal preparation techniques? PART 7 is a guide for your household apothecary table.

PART TWO

A HISTORY OF NATIVE AMERICAN HEALING PRACTICES

The mountains, I become a part of it.
The herbs, the fir tree, I become a part of it.
The morning mists, the clouds, the gathering waters, I become a part of it.
The wilderness, the dew drops, the pollen, I become a part of it.

NAVAJO CHANT

A history of Native American healing practices

When we think of medicine nowadays, most people think of a clinical situation like a hospital or a pharmacy. Still, Jacob reminds us that before the development of "medicine," the plants from which we developed modern medicines were readily available to the many tribes who inhabited the plains, the mountains, and the coasts in North America. There are 574 recognized Native American tribes resident in the US alone. Each tribe adapted to local environments and conditions, including their use of certain herbs, plants, or trees that grew in each region. The ancestors of these tribes traveled from Asia to the Americas over 15,000 years ago.

Aspirin, the most commonly used drug we buy over the counter for headaches, is a compound from the willow tree. It was first processed by Bayer, the German pharmaceutical company, once they recognized its medicinal value. There are "old wives' tales" of nettle tea's use as a tonic, and it has since been proven that the leaves are full of iron and other valuable nutrients that make people happier. Jacob stresses that plants came before modern drugs and that knowledge has largely been lost. But by researching some of the tribes' oral memories, we can utilize plants again for our benefit.

For Native Americans, being healthy includes believing that all of us are part of a universe, each imbued with spirit and a purpose. The ancestors guide our travels, and to maintain health, we must balance the physical and spiritual. The mind must also attune to this universal rhythm. Using locally grown medicines can aid recovery as long as the person undertakes a journey linked to the idea of the interconnection of everything, whether it be the tree outside your window or the daily work you do. This situation is somewhat different from being a patient in a clinical ward. Under the influence of emergency morphine, Jacob found his mind wandering, intrigued by the technology surrounding him but feeling somewhat out of place. Reflecting on what health is, as defined by his grandmother and her tribe, he compared his physical reality to the X-rays, the plaster casts, the physiotherapy, the cheerfulness of the staff, and the sterile rooms of a modern-day hospital. When in the hospital, defining health truly meant its opposite; it was all about disease, illness, and diagnostic tests.

Medicine, supervised by the medical profession, includes diagnosis, checking symptoms, and advising on improving these symptoms. As an X-ray machine scanned Jacob's leg, he recalled how different this was from treatment by his grandmother and her friends. First, they would carefully clean a childhood cut. Then they would dig for cattail roots or available bark or leaves to use and aid recovery. He had fond memories of the antiseptic inside a cattail root tied carefully with the raffia that habitually lived in his grandmother's pockets. Then this strange plaster attached to his leg all the way home flooded back to him. Meanwhile, all the herbs would have been used on the spot or wrapped up carefully in her medicine bag for their safe transportation back to his grandmother's house.

Native American herb collecting is part of a ritual, including offering gifts of thanks by leaving some tobacco, one of the Four Sacred Herbs (along with cedar, sage, and sweetgrass). We enter a sacred space and are permitted to pick just enough for our needs. After giving thanks, it is best to choose the leaves from the eastern side of a tree. Always gather them in the morning, preferably on a sunny day when the sun's energy is smiling down, and the plants are not wilting in the afternoon heat. After the leaves, roots, bark, and stems are collected, they must be stored to avoid damage in transportation, and before leaving, orations are offered to give gratitude for the leaves or part of the plant we have collected. This way, the natural environment does not suffer due to our visit, and enough seeds, leaves, and roots are left until the next stop. Therefore, Native American medicine becomes a complete process that includes our awareness, gratefulness, and protection of the natural environment, which offers us gifts. Compare the difference between a trip to the doctor or specialist in a hospital's sterile surroundings and Native American healthiness. Jacob defines it as not just the opposite of being broken or undamaged and more about becoming "whole," a more holistic approach to health as the connection between belief, lifestyle, nutrition, work, and the environment with the natural world. Being "whole" is a positive overall holistic term for feeling well in mind, body, and spirit. Most traditional doctors also recognize this state as healthy when they see it. It is defining the opposite that can be the problem. Modern medicine admits that there is not necessarily a one size fits all approach to "curing" an illness. Some recover, some don't. Everybody's ability to heal depends on the injury or cause and their mental approach to why they want to recover. Defining the best ways to achieve this depends on the person's will to improve, physical age (young bones heal a lot quicker than older ones!), nutrition, and the underlying unease that "caused" the ill health.

This book does not advise ignoring modern medicine completely. Far from it, it proposes examining the underlying principles of Native American healing that are different from allopathic medicine so that you can adopt the methods you think will bring you back to tip-top health, as defined by you. First, to understand the whole background of the health system of Native Americans, there are certain key tenets of Native American belief to explore.

An introduction to the Native American definition of medicine, health, and wholeness

1. The Medicine Wheel

The Native American Medicine Wheel includes using the four cardinal directions (East, North, West, and South) in a spiritual understanding of their natural world. The modern-day compass is based on a circle of 360 degrees, and the Native American equivalent is the Medicine Wheel; this is hugely important to each tribe. It contributes to the tribal sense of identity, the health and order of the natural world, and an acceptance of following a life in accordance with the spiritual practices passed down from parents to children for thousands of years. Ultimately, this is the touchstone for a healthy life, lived in communion with spirit and body in the modern world.

Also known as the Sacred Hoop or the Circle of Life, the wheel encloses a cross forming four spokes that point in different directions. The center is equally important, and this belief is echoed by other Mesoamerican peoples, such as the Maya and the Aztecs, for whom the World Tree sits in the center.

The number seven is considered sacred in Cherokee teachings. Beyond the four cardinal directions, The Sun above it becomes number five, The Upper World. The roots leading below the ground are number six. Some consider this to be Mother Earth, others that it is The Underground, the life after death, meaning there are six directions so far. The center, or Sacred Fire, unifies and completes the wheel into seven sacred directions, and their connection is vital to understanding Native American beliefs.

The order in which the wheel reads is often counter-clockwise, beginning with East, then North, West, and finally South. Colors assigned to the cardinal directions differ from tribe to tribe. Jacob comments, "My grandmother's tribe placed East as red, the rising sun, and we used to follow the path of the sun in the sky. When it got to midday, the color changed, and the Medicine Wheel altered to blue-white, the midday blinding light (North). Then westward, when the sun starts to set, the color is black, followed by the time of abundance, dreams, and sleep, when the body recovers. The southern part can be white, which represents purity, or green for plants and nature, or sometimes yellow." When physically created or painted, the wheel is depicted as a circle, the whole and never-ending line, a continuous connection that contains all directions and all parts of our lives. Some tribes see it as a wheel, with two emphasized spokes showing the individual components that make all our lives. It serves as a reminder to try to balance all sides of your life, be that family and loved ones, work, or enjoyment, and serves as a reminder to keep all parts of your life in balance.

Large sculptural Medicine Wheels still exist in the wild as sacred places to many Native American tribes. Unfortunately, colonizers and farmers destroyed many. There is one called the Majorville Medicine Wheel located in Alberta, south of Bassano, dated to 3200 BCE (Before Common Era), which means it is over 5,000 years old. A more modern Medicine Wheel was created in 1992 by Joe Stickler in North Dakota, showing two solar calendars: a horizon calendar (The Medicine Wheel) and a meridian or noontime calendar.

2. The Red Path and the Black Road

"The Red Path is the path of good," the path of balance with yourself, your body, your local environment, and nature itself. Described in the Medicine Wheel as the North to South line, this "path" is linked to the idea of a circular environment incorporating East, North, West, and South in the Native American Medicine Wheel. The idea is that no one part of the body (or spirit) exists in isolation. Therefore, if a health problem exists in one part of the body, it is intricately linked to another part of the person's life.

While the Red Path signifies harmony with nature, it is also concerned with generosity and unselfishness. By contrast, the Black Road is the path of warfare and destruction and runs from West to East in the Medicine Wheel. In Native American belief, everybody walks on both, and the goal is to achieve balance by living the best life possible, balancing all needs of each unique personality. Each tribe and nation has its term for this path of good, commonly viewed as balancing the Red Path and the Black Road in one lifetime.

3. Native American healing practices

Traditional Native American ceremonies are an integral part of the process to help promote a greater sense of connection to more profound spiritual and emotional issues. Before the arrival of European colonizers to the Americas, these ceremonies were part of daily life. However, the significant desperation felt by many Native Americans after dislocation and expulsion from their ancestral lands caused a deep wound and a complete change of life for most. Their children were forced into state education and forbidden to speak their native languages. Nevertheless, these healing practices have always been used to restore harmony and joy. Nowadays, they have become a way for tribes to meet while encouraging native language use, dressing in native costumes, chanting, and singing in time to Native American drumming and flutes. In addition, the reintroduction of ancient ceremonies such as Sweat Lodges, Powwows, Pipes, and Herbs brings back wholeness and connection with the planet, which Native American tribes strive to keep alive in our modern world. Let's examine these in more detail.

A. Powwow
B. Music: Dance, Drum, Flute
C. Smudging
D. Storytelling
E. Inipi/Sweat Lodge
F. Pipe Ceremony
G. Herbs

A. POWWOW

A powwow is a community connection where tribes meet in a sacred space combining social interaction with music, drumming, dancing, and wearing a ceremonial dress while always respecting the Creator. These are important occasions in the Native American calendar and occur regularly.

The circular arena in which they occur echoes the shape of the Medicine Wheel and the drum, combining each of the four cardinal directions in a ceremony where Native American drumming, singing, and dancing take place. It emphasizes the holistic wholeness of each action, thought, and word. The understanding is that a powwow brings spiritual renewal with the powerful drumming and chanting, strengthening the connection that Native Americans understand and believe. This idea of solidarity and closeness is reflected in "Mitakuye Oyasin," a Lakota language phrase meaning we are all connected and related.

The origin of the powwow is attributed to the War Dances of tribes of the Southern Plains and the painful memory of Native American public dances enforced by the national government after tribes were forced to live on reservations. Powwow has become a method of combining dancing and musical competitions alongside the parades and the Grand Entry of the Tribes into the circular arena. The discussions of a traditional council also take place. The Grand Entry is the opening ceremony, a showcase of tribal members marching in traditional Native American regalia with whole families parading in a marching spiral shape within the circle. More attendees join through the entrance. The sounds of entire groups of drummers and singers in this enclosed arena are compelling. Younger children are initiated into the opening ceremony wearing outfits handmade by family members.

B. MUSIC: DANCE, DRUM, FLUTE

Dance

Each tribe and nation use dance by wearing decorative headdresses and costumes, and each tribe has its particular dance. Famous dances include the Traditional Dance, the Fancy Dance, the Rain Dance, the Sun Dance, the Corn Dance, the War Dance, and for women, the Jingle Dress Dance. In addition, ancestors are strongly encouraged to participate when these ceremonies occur, linking the present to the past, dancing the same movements for generations.

The Hupa tribe, located in the Hoopa Valley in northwest California, used to perform a Jump Dance, also known as a Redheaded Woodpecker Dance, to renew the world. They wore decorative headdresses adorned with red woodpecker feathers and deerskin robes to bring new energy to heal the earth. The Sun Dance, specifically, is one of the fundamental rites for Oglala Sioux.

Drum

"The rounded shape of the drum is a reminder of the Medicine Wheel, which in itself is a reflection of the physical world with the seasons embedded, its natural cycles, the celestial in the sky, and life after death," comments Jacob. "The whole creation of a drum is based on finding the correct wood and stretching leather from a precious animal, fixed by the skill of the maker and the intention offered to the Creator, imbuing the drum with sacred significance, as the sound is believed to be the heartbeat of the world." The belief that ancestors are also present is a view held among most tribes, and their input is as valuable as the living entity of the planet.

Flute

This Native American instrument is haunting, and when heard in the open spaces for which it was designed, the birdsong echoes the notes as a reminder that the flute is a gift from the Creator. The human voice singing the ancient songs, added to the rhythms connecting with sacred ancestors, brings knowledge from the past to the present, created in the songs and the beat. The flute can be fashioned from native wood and reeds, depending on the location of each particular tribe. For example, flutes could be made from pecan wood in the lower Mississippi valley, whereas red cedar was the choice of tribes within range of this hardwood tree. They loved red cedar for its rich, resonant tone and also a light wood to hold. Cherry wood and maple also offered possibilities, but the scale of difference in terrain where Native Americans lived allowed various types of flutes and drums to be created. The Native American flute has two air chambers and a particular sound, valued worldwide for the tones it achieves.

C. SMUDGING

This ceremony is a way to purify negative thoughts and body energies and invoke ancestors and the spirit to assist in the ceremony. Usually, an herb branch (one of the Four Sacred Herbs) is lit. The resulting smoke and scent allow those seeking purification in the smudging ceremony to inhale and walk through the healing air created. Cedar and sage are burned to eliminate any negative energies. At the same time, sweetgrass is believed to attract positive energy towards the holder of the herb and through them to everybody taking part in the ceremony. Although many individuals create smudging in their homes or workplaces as part of daily meditation practice, many tribes make smudging prayers, asking that their hands be cleansed

to create beauty with them. They ask for their feet to be washed to walk where they most need them. Also, their hearts and throats require purification, and smudging is a prayer to purge the negative, so they can only take positive actions. Smudging is frequently a part of other sacred ceremonies such as Inipi (or Sweat Lodge), which prepare a person and their environment for different spiritual experiences.

D. STORYTELLING

Traditionally, Native American tribes depended on the oral tradition of storytelling as a primary means of passing information from generation to generation. Europeans discovered no known written record when they arrived in the Americas. However, the totem pole tradition is a visual reference to family and ancestors and is easily "read" by Native Americans. The passage of knowledge from parent to child was oral and usually combined storytelling with experience out in the field when an adult collected herbs, trapped animals, or gathered wood. There were also shared storytelling experiences, where the whole tribe gathered, of how the woodpecker had made a hole in a tree branch, and a man blew through the hole, making a noise. Native Americans came to make their flutes in this way. The Spider Woman and Spider Grandmother have their places in many tribal stories, as well as The Woman Who Fell from the Sky.

These stories have tricksters, twins, animals, and birds that transform and speak (such as the coyote and raven). The belief that ancient ancestors could change their bodily form is common in Creation Myths. The stories advise and warn simultaneously about the behavior expected by the tribe. The importance of this oral tradition is indescribable, and the tribes' dislocation from their ancestral lands and traditions has meant that much knowledge has been lost. But, of course, the story of Creation is not the same in any tribe. Still, there are similarities across them all, such as the arrival of the Creator, receiving the Four Sacred Herbs, and sometimes stories were preserved in songs because they would be learned, sung, and repeated and therefore became unforgettable.

E. INIPI OR SWEAT LODGE

Inipi is a ceremony for purification, which is essential before collecting healing herbs and preparing oneself for sacred ceremonies like weddings and ancestral meetings. However, Inipi can also be a ceremony itself, used to calm the mind, body, and spirit. The lodge created varies from tribe to tribe. Branches are cut from local trees and then covered with whatever material is available, ranging from animal skins to foliage to blankets or tarps. The shape of the buildings usually includes a sloping roof with a funnel, but all have an opening to allow sacred herbs to circulate within the lodge and escape. The belief is that the herb smoke escapes above our heads to what the Lakota tribe calls "Up, the realm of the Great Spirit."

Participants typically fast beforehand and sit inside the lodge in a circle close to the heated, steamy stones. A lodge leader guides the ceremony, and a firekeeper heats the 28 stones and splashes them with water to create steam. The vapor scented with the sacred herbs is inhaled deeply by all those in the sweat lodge. The experience is also intricately linked to the four cardinal directions, with the lodge having four doors, each opened and closed, as the lodge leader commences the songs to accompany this. The hot stones and the herbs release steam, which adds to the mystical nature of the ceremony. The Sioux use a circular-shaped lodge, believing its shape is the womb, and the steam rising can reach the Creator above. In the past, the sweat lodge was for only one sex at a time. It was not forbidden for women to participate in the ceremony, but mixed-use was not permitted in most tribes.

Interior of Inipi

Exterior of Inipi

F. PIPE CEREMONY

The Sacred Pipe (sometimes called the Peace Pipe) was used in ceremonies and for personal religious practice by all tribes. The Crow, Omaha, and Pawnee tribes utilized pipes as a prayer combined with dance, making community offerings to the Creator. Contrary to popular belief that tobacco is used in pipe ceremonies, a mixture of red willow and sage is usually preferred. Smoking the sacred tobacco herb was not the pleasure it is to a smoker; rather, it was seen as a praying method, with the rising smoke having the ability to reach the Creator above. As with other ceremonies, participants share the pipe by sitting in a circle, passing the pipe from one person to another. The bowl and pipe are stored separately when not in use. The stem consisted of hardwood, while the pipe bowl contained catlinite when available locally. Also known as pipestone, catlinite is only found in southwestern Minnesota.

The Lakota tribe attributed White Buffalo Cow Woman as the one who gave the gift of the Sacred Pipe. This belief occurs in other tribes that use animals for a particular cardinal direction or seasons, and an individual's Spirit Animal stays with the individual for their lifetime.

G. HERBS

Herbs are the focus of this book. In particular, The Four Sacred Medicines, which include tobacco, cedar, sage, and sweetgrass, were given by the Creator to Native Americans, or so they believe. In Native American belief, a spiritual connection exists between the herb and the collector. Preparing oneself before leaving to collect herbs is part of the ceremony. The collector asks to be provided with the herbs they need, collects them in the prescribed manner, gives thanks, and stores the parts in their medicine bag.

Some healers grow their herbs, which involves careful growing and watchfulness for any problems the plant displays. The herb grower is intimately connected with providing suitable soil with no pesticides, sunshine, and shade, ensuring that the pollinators can find the plant. Giving thanks before and after picking and processing these herbs to conserve their natural goodness is very different from producing healing medicines in a factory plant under controlled conditions.

Many collectors, like Jacob, remember collecting precious herbs in their childhood, and certain tribes believe collection must be early morning when the sun is gaining strength. Jacob describes how his grandmother gave offerings (like tobacco) and thanks to each plant whose leaves were cut. Jacob still has his grandmother's medicine bag, a small, plain hide bag stitched with sinew and a strap worn across her body. It was a suitable receptacle for the sacred offerings from the land she used to heal her family.

Conclusion

Modern medicine offers very useful tools in diagnosis; however, the body tends to be viewed as a machine whose parts require some improvement. The Native American traditions hold the physical body as merely one part of a sacred whole, including the person's mind, spirit, and ancestral connections linked to the environment in which they live. The ceremonies, beliefs, daily spiritual practices, herbs, and traditions will restore a person's life balance.

In PART 3, we will examine why you should feel confident about using Native American herbs.

PART THREE

WHY YOU SHOULD CONSIDER HERBAL REMEDIES

10 reasons to consider herbal medicine before reaching for medically prescribed medications and remedies

1. Herbal medicines work.

There is no doubt that herbal medicines work. Herbs have been used by humanity for a very long time, as evidenced by the contents of stomachs found in the bodies buried in ancient graves all over the world. Aspirin, our most common over-the-counter medicine, is, after all, derived from tree bark originally. In 1978 the scientific advisory board Commission E was established in Germany and approved by the Federal Institute for Drugs and Medicine. This Commission E examined the efficacy of various folk, herbal, and traditional herbal medicines from all over the world and concluded that there was a lot of truth in many natural treatments. As a result, qualified therapists have lists of approved herbals for use in Germany, including herbal oils, lotions, and tinctures, which are referred to worldwide.

Globally, big pharmaceutical companies are investigating plant compounds from which they can extract, synthesize, test, patent, and ultimately sell "new" pharmaceutical drugs, making them enormous profits. Yet, thousands of existing studies around the globe document how effective herbal medicines are for many common or even severe ailments. Broad folk knowledge exists from Asia to Europe to Africa and Australia. It's also the same in the Americas, where Native Americans used herbs and plants to help heal various ailments. Scientific tests confirm the results through antiquities. So, yes, humanity has had extensive knowledge about the medicinal power of herbs for many millennia.

2. Herbal medicines are natural and tend to be safer than pharmaceuticals.

Few people visit a doctor unless they are worried about their symptoms. The doctor may advise that prescribed medicines work well but can cause complications. So, we are prescribed a second pill to counterbalance the first. Many of us look at the information regarding the side effects at our first chance!

Plants taken as herbal mixtures (or certain herb parts) may be eaten, steeped in tea, or applied directly. Following Native American usage, this is a recognized tradition passed down from healer to healer over hundreds of years. However, in laboratory conditions, the complicated process of identifying and separating the compounds from the herb may cause undesired side effects. Therefore, in Native American tradition, healers specify particular parts of the herb, used correctly and taken correctly. Certain herbs are not recommended for use by pregnant women because they may stimulate the womb to contract, or by new mothers for fear of breast milk drying up. However, these effects are common knowledge among herb specialists – please see a list at the end of PART 5. You must check with your herbalist and medical practitioner before usage. Herbal medicines used correctly will provide safe, natural remedies and alternatives to processed over-the-counter drugs.

3. Herbal medicines are affordable.

For centuries, monastery gardens provided cooks with herbs for flavoring and physicians with particular leaves, seeds, flowers, and roots to ease medical disorders. Picking herbs is usually free, and making herbal oils takes a little time, but both can be done quickly and easily (see PART 7 for details). In addition, you can grow herbal medicines in your backyard.

Pharmaceutical companies need to cover their lengthy development costs while testing the efficiency and safety of commercial drugs. However, it is increasingly evident that profit is often a factor, and frequently, drug prices soar as the need becomes more significant. One example of this is how we have access to insulin. It was released for free to the medical profession by its inventor, but today you'll find the price regularly increasing for the patient by the major drug companies.

On the other hand, natural homegrown herbs provide affordable health care, and you can also be confident that no artificial chemicals are used in their cultivation.

4. Herbal medicine is sustainable medicine.

Pharmaceutical companies have a poor record of environmental damage and high health system costs. Suppose we can restructure society to cultivate herbs on balconies, back gardens, or even in local public gardens and parks. In that case, it may be possible to provide people with sustainable alternatives to prescription drugs that they can grow themselves. Local medicines and the need for adequate knowledge of the correct plant parts can benefit the environment and health.

Many studies show that gardeners are among the most relaxed and content individuals. Many see caring for their plants as part of the role in healing. The cultivation of herbs may provide exercise, a connection to nature, and a naturally resourced pharmacy. Herbalists are also environmentally conscious and keen to source plants grown free of pesticides.

Since plants can be grown in remote environments, and doctors and prescriptions may be many miles away, herbal medicine must be cultivated and brought back into mainline knowledge. If growing herbs and using them locally relieves common ailments, we can improve health. As a result, local communities become powerful in providing their much-needed medicinal solutions.

5. Most herbs contain innumerable healing compounds.

Laboratory examination reveals that herbs contain various compounds. When the herb is eaten or steeped as tea, fewer side effects are noticed than when isolated compounds are taken in pills and tablets. Herb tinctures (where the concentrated herb is preserved in alcohol for use when required – see PART 7) and herbal teas use the whole, medicinal parts of the plant rather than a single compound isolated in a laboratory.

6. Herbal medicines and pharmaceuticals may interact.

Unless the medical profession gets involved, doctors tend to be cynical about herbs; after all, they are both medicines. So, checking with your doctor or qualified herbalist before taking both is essential. There are particular examples of herbs, such as feverfew, which should not be taken during the five days before surgery as it is an anticoagulant. Professional herbalists and practitioners will be aware of this. Still, many doctors will not, so discussing any medications or herbal preparations you take with your doctor before surgery is essential.

7. Herbs used in cooking can retain their benefits.

Often people classify herbs as either for cooking or medicine, but in reality, there is a tremendous amount of crossover. In other words, many herbs we regularly use in food also have excellent healing properties and vice versa. For example, garlic is known to help lower blood pressure and provide a pleasant taste to food.

8. You should not use herbs in the same way you use other drugs.

We take a specific drug for a particular symptom of illness in the pharmaceutical world. However, herbs work differently; they strengthen the body from the inside out. Therefore, it may take longer to notice the improvement of symptoms because they are not going to the root of the problem first. Instead, they keep the entire body strong, including the source of illness.

9. Ensure you are using the correct plant.

Be well-informed, check which part is to be used, and harvest it in optimum conditions. For instance, Jacob collects in the sunshine in the morning hours. Other tribes had routines and practices to ensure the plant is given thanks and is picked respectfully. Be conscious that different varieties of herbs exist depending on where you live. For example, oregano is a name given to many plants. Check the scientific name of the plant you are interested in and go with a guide or have good photographic references to verify it before picking.

10. Make sure to use the correct part of the plant.

Before you set out, check a plant reference guide and check if it is leaf, seed, flower, root, or bark to be collected, and only pick what you need. Some plant parts may be toxic if ingested, whereas they work perfectly on the skin in an ointment.

So why are some doctors so against alternative medicine?

Medical doctors spend many years in college and in medical settings. They may perceive herbalists and Native American practitioners as lacking these years of study and experience. However, the manner of the doctor, and the patient's experience with doctors, is often why holistic medicine and herbalists are so popular. Patients sometimes complain that doctors do not have enough time during an appointment to listen or that they only search for symptoms. In medical journals, "alternative" medicine is considered "unproven." However, the US Pharmacopeia and Commission E in Germany have scientifically investigated and found reputable and valuable herbs in health care. The US Pharmacopeia describes itself as "an independent, scientific nonprofit organization focused on building trust in the supply of safe, quality medicines."

Many prescribed medicines have harmful side effects, and a patient must consider whether the drug suits them. The herbs included in this book have no harmful effects if used correctly. It would be helpful for doctors to investigate herbal benefits while bearing in mind that medical treatments or procedures cause 25% of US hospital admissions. Some doctors have begun to refer patients to herbalists and other alternative therapists because patients want this choice.

However, it would be best if you remember that the Food and Drug Administration has not evaluated the herbs in this book. Jacob makes no medical claims nor intends to diagnose, treat, or heal medical conditions. Pregnant women or those with known medical conditions should always consult their physicians before trying herbal remedies for common ailments.

A final word from Jacob

Remember that collecting herbs is a sacred task, and give thanks for what the plant offers to you. Collect when the sun is warm on your back, and you are in a positive mindset. Never pick too much from one plant; take small amounts and store the selected pieces carefully.

Eleven popular herbs are introduced in detail in PART 4, and comprehensive information about 101 herbs is provided in PART 5. Common ailments are listed in PART 6 with the herbs recommended for treating that ailment, with a guidebook for preparation in PART 7. Please enjoy.

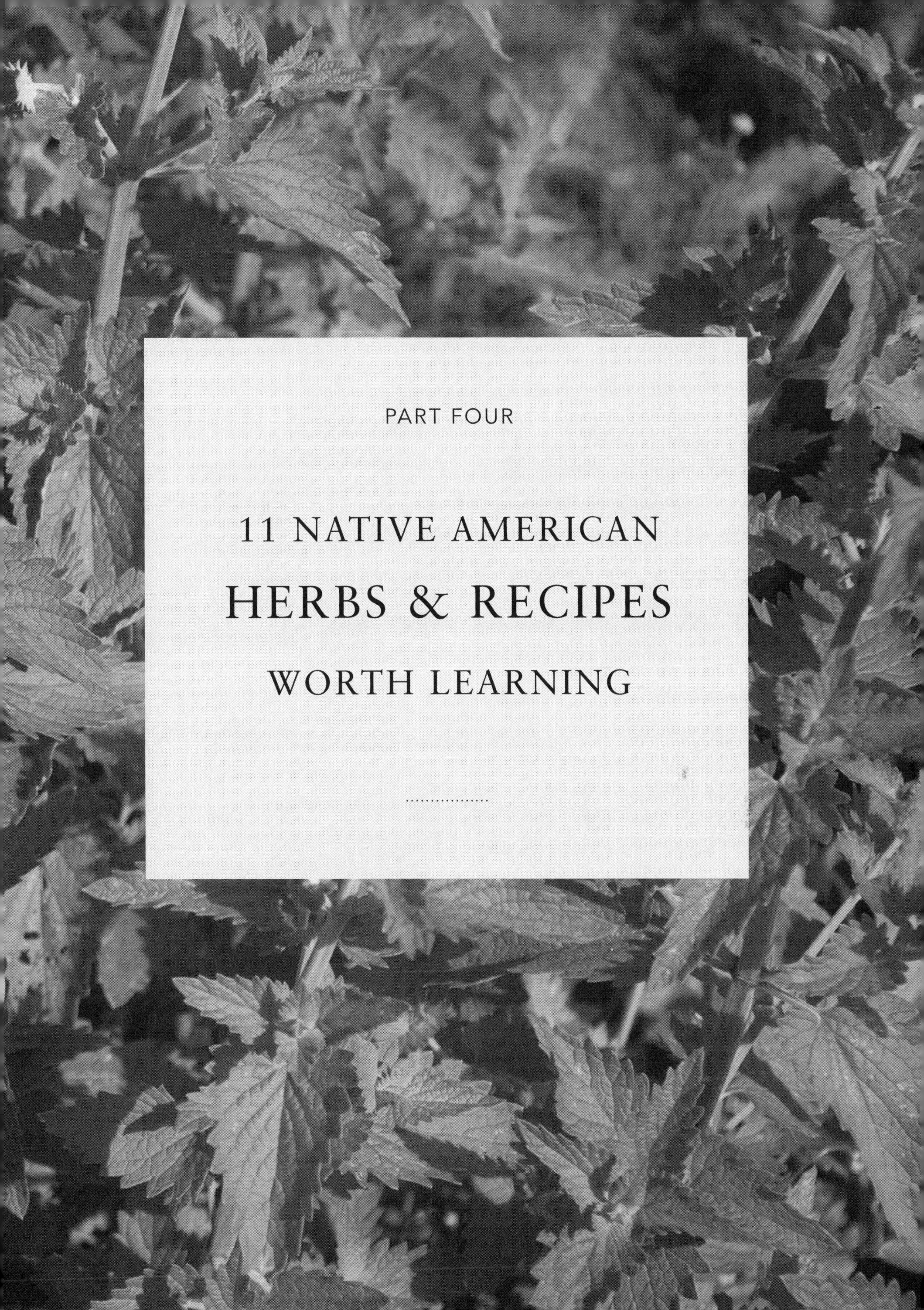

PART FOUR

11 NATIVE AMERICAN HERBS & RECIPES WORTH LEARNING

"All plants are our brothers and sisters. They talk to us, and if we listen, we can hear them."

ARAPAHO PROVERB

11 Native American herbs & recipes worth learning

1. Blackberry
2. Buckbrush
3. Cattail
4. Dandelion
5. Elderflower
6. Flaxseed
7. Mint
8. Rosemary
9. Sage
10. Sumac
11. Yarrow

General hints for harvesting herbs

Before you begin, putting yourself in the right frame of mind is essential. Jacob reminds us that collecting herbs is a sacred task. The plants offer parts of their flowers, stems, leaves, and roots for our benefit. Giving gratitude and leaving gifts (as his grandmother taught him) is vital. Tobacco is a traditional gift, and a verbal thank you to the plant is required.

Choosing a good day to harvest herbs is also crucial, so check the weather forecast. If you are collecting in the wild, try to ensure that your plants are not on roadside verges that may have had weed killer or chemicals used. Collect herbs in the morning while the sun rises in the sky, as the herbs you pick may wilt in the hottest afternoon sunshine. Remember only to collect every third plant. This Native American rule ensures that the plants thrive, even if you take some for your use.

Conserve the herb carefully until your arrival home, and then place herbs in the shade if you are drying them for winter use. While each herb's storage details are provided in this section, see instructions for drying and using in PART 7.

1. Blackberry. *Latin name: Rubus villosus*

The blackberry plant has been known and used by humanity for centuries. Ropes of plaited reddish-colored blackberry roots have been found in Native American graves and other civilizations worldwide. Native Americans used blackberries as a tonic for sore throats and coughs. They also used the leaves, stems, and roots for their other health benefits.

What to use blackberry for

Food: Eat fruit for nutrition. Harvested worldwide as a tasty black fruit, blackberries contain vitamins A, B, C, E, and K, and potassium, magnesium, calcium, manganese, and polyphenols.

Cough mixture: Native American use of berries or roots as a cough mixture is widespread – see the recipe further on.

Toothache: Many tribes used blackberry leaves to chew on, which helped relieve toothache pain. Yarrow was also used (see no. 11 later in this section).

Stomach upsets: Use the leaves as a tea for stomach upsets, and boil the root and leaves together for diarrhea.

Disease prevention: In terms of disease prevention, some research suggests that the manganese in blackberries may help prevent osteoporosis. Consumption of its polyphenols may lower the risk of diabetes because these tend to lower blood sugar levels. Jacob comments that diabetes in Native American populations was almost unknown. Still, since they have adopted the American way of life, the levels of diabetes have climbed at the same rate as everybody else.

What part of the plant do I collect?

Pick the berries when they turn from red to black, generally in late summer. They are high in vitamin C, and a cup of blackberries provides one of your five daily dietary requirements.

You can brew the leaves into a blackberry tea. First, pick the leaves, dry them, add a few to a cup, and add boiling water. Then, allow the leaves to steep for 5 minutes, remove them from the tea, and enjoy. See drying techniques in PART 7.

Use the roots for stomach upsets. Harvest roots in the fall or spring when the plant is almost dormant. Remove a small amount of the root for your use, ensuring the plant has been left with enough material to continue to survive. Make sure you don't take the whole root! Wash them well and cut into small pieces. Boil them with the leaves and bark of the bush to make a tonic for stomach upsets. Roots can be dried, cut into smaller pieces, and ground into powder in a food processor for winter use.

When do I collect blackberries?

If you have young children or grandchildren, ask them to collect the berries with you for a fun family activity. Then, collect some windfall apples if you can, as they will add sweetness to the taste.

Blackberries are harvested in late summer to early fall when the berries are dark black. You can pick leaves in any season, but all herbs are best picked in the early morning on a sunny day. Roots are best dug in the fall when the plant dies back for winter. However, if you need some during winter, remember where the plant is and dig a small amount for use.

How do I store blackberries?

Freeze the berries for winter use. First, dig up a portion of the roots and allow them to dry naturally or in the oven at low heat. Then cut and grind the pieces in a food processor and store this powder in a jar or the freezer.

How to grow blackberries

Carefully! These plants take over large spaces rapidly, as you will know if you go blackberry picking, so confine them to one location with fences and remove suckers as they try to spread. Dig a hole to fit the plant's root ball and cover it with nutritious soil with plenty of humus and organic matter. The better the growing medium, the more fruit you can pick! Firm the ground a little with your fingers and water the plant well. If there is not much rain during the spring or fall when you are planting, check how dry the soil is and occasionally give it water with a watering can. Once the plant is established, blackberries usually don't need watering unless it is an arid summer.

Blackberries grow everywhere in the wild. They are almost invasive in woodland, but if you want to grow them in your garden, Jacob's tips are as follows. First, they require lots of room to grow in full sun. The plant will grow to fit any space you give it and produces suckers (mini plants with roots), so remove these if you don't want them to take over your whole garden. It is a good idea to root a new sucker into a plant pot every 3-4 years, as, in nature, the plant spreads and the soil may become depleted. If you root a sucker plant in a container, you can cut it off from the host plant and transplant it into a new space after a few years.

Add some manure and homemade compost every year in spring to give it lots of richness, then carefully make a hole bigger than the root ball of your plant.

How to make blackberry miracle cough and cold syrup (formerly used for whooping cough)

Be sure to use a cup to measure quantities. Start with 4 cups (0.95 l) of fresh berries, 1 teaspoon of ground cinnamon, 1 teaspoon of cloves, and enough water to cover the fruit (at least 4 cups (0.95 l)). Sometimes Jacob adds an apple or two if there is plenty of fruit falling. Remove the apples' skin and add them to the fruit mixture.

If you prefer a tonic with a bitter taste, add 1 cup (0.24 l) of vinegar to the pan. If you like your mixture sweet, honey has good antiseptic qualities. So you can add a cup of honey, but save adding it until the berries have fully cooked.

Bring the ingredients to a boil and keep the pan at high heat to soften the berries.

After 10 minutes, reduce the heat and top up with water if the mixture is not covered.

Allow the mixture to bubble away, stir it from time to time, and your berries should be ready in about 40 minutes. Next, use a food mill or processor to reduce the mixture to a smooth consistency.

Strain through a fine sieve to remove seeds, cloves, and cinnamon, and return the mixture to the saucepan. Add the honey now if you want to use it. Keep stirring until the honey has been mixed in thoroughly. Adding honey is highly recommended if children are taking this tonic!

How to take the blackberry tonic for sore throats

Take two teaspoons every 4 hours to help relieve the roughness and sore throat a chesty cough brings. You can take one or two teaspoons directly, add the tonic to some hot water as a hot drink, or even spoon it over ice cream or desserts.

2. Buckbrush. *Latin name: Symphoricarpos orbiculatus*

This plant is known as coralberry and Indian currant, which refers to its pink berries. A pretty addition to your garden, it will add yellowish-white flowers in spring, green leaves all summer, and a splash of pink berries in the fall. It is a favorite grazing plant for deer, so if you have some locally, make sure this plant is out of their reach!

What to use buckbrush for

Respiratory issues: A tea from the roots is beneficial to soothe and reduce the inflammation of sore throats and to treat fevers and catarrh. Dig up a small root, wash it carefully, and add it to boiling water to make the tea. When the liquid cools, drink a cup and save the rest in a sealed container to help with that sore throat.

Basketry: Making baskets with this plant was its primary use by the Cherokees.

What part of the plant do I collect?

The roots are the best way to consume it by using it as tea.

How do I store buckbrush?

Dig up some roots before the ground gets too frosty and dry them indoors to store for winter use. Wash them, cut into small pieces, and allow them to dry on a piece of paper. When completely dry, store them in an airtight jar to use whenever you require them.

How to grow buckbrush

This perennial, evergreen shrub is common in gardens in Texas, Florida, and right through to Colorado and South Dakota in the US. It also grows happily in the wild and is loved by bees and butterflies, so you will have plenty of wildlife to admire wherever you place the bush. It is a member of the buckthorn family and can grow to a significant size. So when planting the shrub, you should allow for some expansion. At its tallest, it is likely to shade other plants, so you will need to prune the bush back in a domestic garden from time to time. Buckbrush prefers a position in full sun with fertile soil.

3. Cattail. *Latin Name: Typha*

Cattails were very important to many tribes because of their versatility as a food plant and for ceremonies. Cattails grow freely in fresh or brackish water with some salinity, like estuaries and riversides with tidal areas. Besides being edible, the Pueblo tribes used cattails in ceremonial rain dances. For the Navajo, it was believed the cattail could protect against storms and lightning. Cattail pollen was used in face painting; if you touch it, you will see why! The color is intense, and the texture is clearly defined against the skin. In Europe, a similar plant called a bulrush plant can survive dry summers in wetland areas. However, cattails choose shallower water than bulrushes. Cattails grow from rhizome roots which spread in any place where they grow, and they are adored by wildlife, providing cover and nesting areas. However, nowadays, they are also grown ornamentally, and their leaves are used in basketry by some tribes. The Osage tribe adopted the cattail as their clan symbol.

What to use cattails for

Food: Cattail heads provided as much carbohydrate as potatoes and were eaten as food.

Pain: Joint pain and stomach aches were said to be eased by an infusion of the roots.

First aid: Cattail roots were used for emergency wound care in many Native American health-care regimes.

Pillow stuffing: The soft material of the heads was used as lining in moccasins and stuffing for pillows.

Basketry: Basketry and weaving required leaves from the common cattail (Typha latifolia).

Face painting: Using cattails provided a natural coloring without any additives. However, this is not recommended for trick-or-treating. Native American usage was always to use a little of any plant and use it with gratitude.

What part of the plant do I collect?

Native Americans used the roots as an antiseptic for cuts and open injuries. First, they dug up a small amount of root (enough to cover the wound), ensuring that the affected area was cleaned of dirt, using water to do this first. Next, they cut open or split it and secured the antiseptic qualities of the root using raffia from plants or any available string or rope.

Cook the roots as food by boiling, baking, or barbecuing.

Boil the roots to make an infusion.

The catkins are the young shoots that will become the head, but this part can be eaten like corn on the cob if cut early.

The heads are edible, but you must pick them before they go to seed.

The leaves and stems are still used for making floor mats, chair seats, weaving, and basketry.

When do I collect cattails?

Pick roots when needed in any season. The antiseptic qualities come only from the living plant, so do not pick it for use later. Indoors you will use your standard first aid kit, so cattail is for emergency wound cleaning only. If you want to eat the roots, pick them when the plant has fully grown in the fall or the winter. The roots are full of goodness. They can be boiled, grilled, and baked, or you can even make cattail flour. You can pick leaves in any season, but it is more practical in the summer or when the heads are in season. Try to harvest your leaves early in the morning on a sunny day and dry them for use later.

Catkins (the young shoots) can be picked in spring and eaten like corn on the cob. If you harvest the catkins at this stage, the head will not have formed, but be careful not to remove all of them. Make sure you leave plenty of shoots to produce mature heads for later use.

How do I store cattails?

Pick cattails as fresh as you can when they are required. They are challenging to store because the antiseptic qualities are only in the fresh herb, so use cattails as an emergency first aid kit when out in the countryside.

How to grow cattails

They can be grown in a pond or a stream if you have access to one. You will need a root (rhizome) to plant in shallow water, where it will spread over time.

4. Dandelion. *Latin name: Taraxacum officinale*

The harbinger of spring, this sunshiny-yellow flower is nectar for bees early in the pollen season. It has become a wish flower for many children, blowing their wishes as the seed heads fly into the distance. Some Native American tribes, including the Cherokee and the Iroquois, chewed on dandelion leaves to ease a sore tooth. The

Cherokee also used an infusion of the root to cleanse the blood and an infusion of the leaves to calm nervousness. The Ojibwa drank dandelion tea for heartburn, and other tribes used the tea as a health tonic. This usage is borne out medically by knowledge of the contents of dandelion leaves. Brewed as a tea, they are a remedy used worldwide to treat kidney problems, heartburn, and swelling.

The Navajo used a poultice of leaves or made an infusion and used these to soothe sore eyes. The Aleut placed a poultice of steamed leaves around the neck for sore throats. The Bella Coola in British Columbia used a decoction of the root for stomach pains. All plant parts can be utilized (apart from the seeds), from the bright yellow flowers the bees love in early spring to the long tap roots that dig deep into the soil, extracting goodness from layers below. Gardeners use its leaves as a fertilizer, soaked in water, to encourage tomato growth. This "weed" is part of the medical folklore of Europe, Asia, and worldwide for the benefits it brings.

What to use dandelion for

Sore throats: Dandelion salad (made with fresh, new leaves), according to Native American belief, can help soothe a tickly, sore throat.

Flush out toxins: Dandelion tea (made from leaves) is a known diuretic that causes you to flush out toxins. However, too much tea will have you visiting the toilet all night, so limit yourself to one or two cups daily.

Sore muscles: Make dandelion oil from the flowers and rub this on aching muscles after exercise.

Detoxify the liver: Use the leaves to make dandelion tea to cleanse the system when water retention is a problem. Also helpful for the gallbladder.

Get rid of warts: When you crush the flower's stem, the sap that escapes is said to get rid of warts if applied regularly.

Coffee substitute: Dandelion roots can be used as a coffee substitute, not for the taste, but as a hot drink alternative.

Eat the flowers and leaves: Dandelion flowers were used to flavor homemade wine, and you can add them to salads for a colorful new taste, being rich in vitamins A and C. The plant is from Europe, but has made its way to all of the Americas and Asia. Traditionally, it was used by the Cherokee as a tonic to purify the blood.

What part of the plant do I collect?

The flowers are entirely edible, so they can be added to salads, made into wine, or oil infused with flowers to ease aches and pains. See the recipe further on.

Leaves, picked when fresh and young, can be eaten raw, in salads, and made into tea. Older leaves taste bitter, like spinach, and must be cooked for 5-10 minutes.

Stem sap has been used to treat warts for centuries. Squeeze the stem and apply the residue directly to any skin wart.

The roots make a dandelion coffee substitute. They go very deep into the soil, extracting valuable minerals and organic matter not accessible to other plants, and that is why the leaves and roots are so full of goodness! Jacob emphasizes that this drink does not taste like coffee, but if you want a replacement hot drink, this is your plant. Dig up only every third plant in the Native American way of harvesting, to allow the plant to continue growing during the following season. Dandelions are prolific seeders and will rise again even if you leave the tiniest amount of growth. So don't be greedy; only pick as much as you need.

When do I collect dandelions?

Roots are harvested in the fall to take full advantage of the plants' growing season. Pick all your leaves, flowers, and roots when the sun rises, as your energy is at its best.

Leaves should be collected when they are young but before flowering, if possible. Otherwise, the older leaves can taste quite bitter if eaten raw. The leaves contain vitamins A, B, C, D, and K and have iron, magnesium, potassium, and zinc traces.

How do I store dandelions?

Store freshly picked leaves in a bag in the fridge. They are best eaten fresh, but they will last two days or so in the refrigerator. Dry the leaves for use in tea during the winter months.

How to grow dandelions

Dandelions do not usually need to be seeded, as they are often the scourge of lawns! They like a bright, sunny location with lots of fertile soil. Gather seeds from a flower already gone to seed – the "puffball" children love to blow – and allow these to settle on freshly dug soil. Cover them lightly with earth. They will grow happily from spring through fall without your intervention. Be warned that they will spread everywhere you grow them, so try to put them in one location and remove seed heads to avoid annoyance to neighbors' gardens.

How to make dandelion oil for muscle strain and pain relief

Find a recycled glass container and add a handful of flowers, freshly picked with stems cut off. Next, fill the jar with your chosen oil; use any you prefer. For example, olive oil offers a neutral flavor, and almond oil is sweeter. Add a lid and then place the jar in an area away from direct sunlight for about two weeks. The flowers will add a golden glow to your oil, which can be decanted into a clean jar and stored in the fridge. Great for use on aching muscles after sports or any activity!

5. Elderflower. *Latin Name: Sambucus nigra*

Elder trees grow tall and shade large areas with foliage. The flowers and berries are consumed as food, as syrups for colds, and the flowers make a delightful, refreshing summer drink. Elderflowers can be used in tea for a delicious taste and have a soothing effect on the eyes when used in eye lotions. The flowers add a unique flavor to cordials, wines, and even elderflower champagne, popular in the UK. Elderflower tea will soothe a sore throat, and dried flower tea is helpful in winter, along with the elderberry tonic made from the fruit. See the recipe further on.

What to use elderflower for

Sore throats, colds, and flu: Elderberry syrup is taken to soothe sore throats and recover from bronchitis, coughs, colds, and flu. Because the berries are very high in vitamin C, you can make the leaves into a decoction to gargle for a sore throat. So if you are a teacher used to talking all day, this is the natural remedy!

Parkinson's Disease: The Lumbee of North Carolina use elderberries to treat the symptoms of this disease.

Food: Elderflowers can be dipped in batter and fried to make a gorgeous dessert.

Drinks: Elderflower tea is a refreshing summer drink. Also, elderflower cordial and lemonade are enjoyed wherever elderflowers grow.

Lotions: Elderflowers' soothing qualities make them a popular ingredient for eyewashes and ointments.

Constipation: Extract of elderflower is helpful as a temporary aid. If the condition continues, eat more vegetables and fruit and chat with your medical adviser.

Mumps: Elderberry has antiviral properties that can be useful to soothe the symptoms associated with mumps.

What part of the plant do I collect?

Flowers can be collected in May and sometimes June when the pollen is still visible.

You can boil the leaves into a decoction and then gargle for a sore throat.

Berries should be picked fresh in the fall when they are full or bursting, but it is too late if they are shriveled like a dried raisin.

When do I collect elderflowers?

Flowers arrive from May onwards and should not be picked on a rainy day because the famous smell will have washed off! The flowers need pollen on them, which provides that gorgeous smell. Pick them on a sunny day and do not wash them before drying or using them.

Pick berries in early fall, when they are black and whole, not dried and wilted.

Leaves can be picked in any season, but they are best harvested early in the morning on a sunny day.

How do I store elderflower?

Flowers: Pick them fresh off the tree to make lemonade and cordial or elderflower fritters. You can dry the entire flower umbels (clusters) but remove the stalks when storing them, or you will have them in your tea. Store the flowers in a dark cupboard away from direct sunlight and replace the flowers every year.

Berries: Make elderberry tonic as soon as the berries are ripe and store it in bottles for winter use. You can also freeze the berries for use throughout the winter.

How to grow elderflower

Elderflower is a tree, not a shrub, and it is best to select one with no risk of roadside pollution. The elderflower trees can grow as tall as 30 feet (9.14 m) in your garden, so ensure you place your young plant in a sunny position. It enjoys full sun and will provide shelter for birds who love to nest in the taller branches. Cats love to scratch on elder bark too.

How to make elderberry syrup

Pick handfuls of berries when they ripen from green to black and feel soft to the touch. Unfortunately, they are quite bitter to taste, although some people like them raw.

Remove the stalks, add them to a saucepan with enough water to cover the fruit, and bring it to a boil. You will notice seeds in the mixture, so strain the liquid to remove them.

Combine 2 cups (about 500 ml) of the mixture with 1 ½ cups (350 g) of sugar and the juice of one squeezed lemon. If you like ginger, add a small piece at this stage. It has active ingredients (gingerol and shogaol), which add extra taste and help against colds and sore throats.

Allow the mixture to cook gently on low heat and stir to ensure the sugar has dissolved. Then cool the mixture, strain the ginger and spices, and store in a sterilized container away from direct light. You can also freeze the mix to use in small doses when required.

6. Flaxseed. *Latin name: Linum usitatissimum*

Flax is a beautiful blue flower in any garden display, and you can harvest its seeds for oil and eat them once they're dried. In Europe, the plant was used to make linen, while Native Americans used the seeds to soothe sore throats and help kidney function. More recently, a study investigated the regular consumption of flaxseed in Native American postmenopausal women and found it lowered cholesterol and positively affected lipid profiles, thereby reducing their risk of cardiovascular disease. In addition, flaxseed contains healthy lignans, omega-3 fatty acids, and fiber.

What to use flaxseed for

Sore throats: Flaxseed can be made into a soothing syrup (see the recipe later on).

Kidneys: Flaxseed is recommended for people with kidney problems.

Heart health: Reports say that using 30 g per day lowers cholesterol and reduces heart disease risk.

What part of the plant do I collect?

Seeds are helpful for sore throats and are often recommended for people with heart concerns as they add vital nutrients. However, it is essential not to eat raw flaxseed – they must be ripe and dried if you are collecting them at home.

You can also consume flaxseed in any way you see fit (sprinkled on cereal, added to bread mixes, or in cookies) so long as you do not take it when it's raw or unripe. You can also dry the seeds and grind them into powder, which is an excellent way to store them.

When do I collect flaxseed?

Collect the ripe, brown seeds on a sunny day early in the morning. It is important not to eat fresh seeds; they need to be dried to get the full benefits. Flaxseed oil releases all the goodness, too, so use the oil in cooking.

How do I store flaxseed?

Seeds can be picked and then dried on a sheet of paper. Some growers like to hang the whole plant upside down indoors, but this requires a lot of space, and you can simply harvest them into an envelope or use greaseproof paper in an oven that has finished baking potatoes. After drying, store them in a sterilized jar. You can then press them to make oil, which is quite a laborious process but very satisfying if you have the time.

How to grow flaxseed

Rake your soil and remove any perennials like dandelions. Flax enjoys some compost added, and if you have manure, that allows them to flourish. Their gorgeous blue flowers will bring eye-catching color to your garden, and the seeds form shortly afterward. These plants grow tall from 12-24 inches (approximately 30-60 cm), and giving them a sunny spot with some shelter will pay dividends. Flaxseeds are tiny and will fly in the wind, so plant them on a day when there is not a strong breeze. Keep them in the packet until the soil is ready, and then pour them out of the pack carefully. These plants are reasonably frost-hardy, but do not plant them too early, or they will just sit in wet soil. They are best planted when the ground is warming up in spring. Dig and rake the dirt, then scatter the seeds. The area needs to be watered well, then covered with an inch (2.5 cm) of soil or compost. Keep an eye on the ground through the spring as they grow, and water them occasionally in dry periods. When the seed heads form, it is good to stop watering to encourage the seeds to form and dry. You can pick the dry seed heads by cutting the stalks and shaking them into an envelope to harvest. If you prefer to dry them indoors, pick the stems and hang them upside down in a shady spot. Then gather the seeds into a sterilized container once dry.

How to make flaxseed cough syrup

Boil 2 tablespoons (30 g) of flaxseeds in 1 cup (0.24 l) of water until it becomes thick. Strain carefully, squeeze the moisture from the mulch, and add 3 tablespoons (44 g) each of honey and lemon juice. Stir thoroughly and decant into a sterilized container.

7. Mint. *Latin name: Mentha arvensis*

Well-known for its digestive properties, both the Shosone and the Paiute made teas from dried stems and leaves to help ease flatulence. It was used as a pneumonia treatment by the Menominee, and most Eastern tribes inhaled the steam from mint in boiling water to ease many respiratory problems, a practice still common today. The Lakota favored it as a headache treatment, by creating an infusion from the leaves or the roots.

In many cultures like Greece, mint is the herb of choice. Peppermint tea is a Mediterranean favorite, and as we all know, it is used in toothpaste for the fresh taste it adds to the mouth. It is often provided at the end of a meal for this reason, and to avoid flatulence. Pick leaves when you need them, and you can also dry mint leaves for winter usage when the plant has died back (mint dies back entirely in winter, so pick leaves before this happens).

What to use mint for

To cool down: Drink refreshing peppermint tea on a hot day, and you will feel cooler. Its use can also help bring down a fever. When left to get cold, it can be soaked into a flannel cloth and used to massage hot foreheads.

Diarrhea: Use a decoction – see PART 7 for how to do this.

Flatulence: Fresh mint is frequently served after meals as a refreshing mouthwash, as well as to relieve any flatulence problems which may have appeared.

Insect repellent: Insects hate the smell of mint, and rodents also dislike it, so grow mint where you do not want these creatures.

Stomach upsets: The Cherokee made mint tea to soothe indigestion and calm an upset stomach.

Itching: Make a salve from the leaves to relieve itching skin and rashes. See the recipe further on.

Respiratory problems: An infusion can help with colds, congestion, bronchitis, and pneumonia symptoms.

What part of the plant do I collect?

Collect the leaves to be used fresh or dried and roots to make a decoction.

When do I collect mint?

Pick leaves when you need them in spring and summer. But remember, if you want a mint supply for the winter, you must dry some of the leaves you've gathered. Pick a few branches at intervals throughout the summer months when the plant is thriving and hang these upside down in a shady area to dry. When the leaves feel dry to the touch, store them in an airtight spice jar for use in winter.

How do I store mint?

Dried leaves will keep in a spice jar all winter. You can save new leaves the following season and repeat the storage process.

How to grow mint

You will find that bees and butterflies flock to your mint plant, so you can enjoy the buzzing sound in the summer. Plant mint in spring or fall; don't worry when it disappears in winter. Make sure your mint plant has its roots contained because this herb loves to spread and can become invasive. Add a layer of compost, leaf mold, or manure once a year in spring to nourish the herb during the growing season. Mint tends to deplete the soil after about three years, so remember to dig up your herb, divide the roots, and give it a new lease on life. In the wild, mint will keep spreading to find newly enriched soil.

How to make a mint salve

Pick ¼ cup (25 g) of the fresh herb and add it to 2 cups (0.47 l) of olive or sunflower oil in a saucepan. Simmer at low heat for an hour. Allow this mixture to cool, strain the liquid into a sterilized jar, and seal. Apply this mixture to soothe and relax aching muscles from sporting activities.

8. Rosemary. *Latin name: Salvia rosmarinus*

Rosemary is a perennial, aromatic shrub used by Native Americans to ease muscle pain. The leaves can be cooked and crushed into an ointment, adding a delicious scent to any healing remedy. It is a powerful herb, so use it sparingly in cooking and healing. Its delicious taste makes it a popular spice in cooking, not only for Native Americans, but also worldwide.

What to use rosemary for

Pain relief: Rosemary has been shown to reduce pain in conditions like neuralgia and can be used to relieve soreness in muscles and joints. It is often combined with lavender in healing ointments.

Cooking: A sprig of rosemary can be added to stews and casseroles, where the scent will infuse your dish with flavor over a slow cooking period. Just remember to remove it before serving. In Mediterranean recipes, rosemary complements lamb, pork, and veal and adds depth of flavor to vegetarian meals.

Massage oil: Rosemary leaves added to a massage oil will significantly relieve muscles and joints after a hard day. However, be careful with using it while pregnant. Best to avoid it, and seek advice from your physician concerning any unexpected reactions. For jaundice sufferers, the oil can be massaged topically on to the liver area.

What part of the plant do I collect?

Leaves can be picked whenever you like. This herb is perennial and will have fresh foliage in every season. Pick the fresh rosemary leaves for immediate use, or dry them for winter use if you prefer.

When do I collect rosemary?

Pick the leaves whenever you need them from a shrub growing outdoors. However, traditionally, herbs are best collected in the morning if planning an evening meal. In winter, rosemary will hibernate like most plants, and you may worry if frost appears to kill off the growing tips. However, this herb will bounce back in spring as the cold will not damage the roots.

How do I store rosemary?

Dry your pruned branches by tying them upside down in a shady spot indoors, and then pick off the dried leaves and store them in a spice jar. The smell will also permeate the area of your home where you hang the branches. Use rosemary leaves in herb oil, as the scent is long-lasting. You can add it to bath oil for a refreshing scent and moisturizer.

How to grow rosemary

Rosemary can be grown from seed in May or June, but it will take several years before your shrub is big enough to pick its leaves. The soil does not need to be very rich, but you will need to initially water a new plant very well. Once established, it will do okay with rainwater. Rosemary loves a sunny spot and will thrive if you have a south-facing wall. Because it can grow up to 2 feet (0.61 m) high, allow enough space around your plant for it to expand. Rosemary has beautiful blue flowers, so place it where you can enjoy them in summer. Also, pollinating bees adore them. Rosemary can get quite leggy, so prune it every year and use these branches to dry herbs for winter.

How to make rosemary and lavender ointment

Pick some sprigs of both herbs and use 1 tablespoons (25 g) of each. Add them with 1 pint (0.47 l) of olive or sunflower oil in a saucepan. Simmer on low heat for 1 ½ hours or so, adding water if needed. Allow the mixture to cool, strain the liquid into a sterilized jar, and seal. Apply this mixture to soothe and relax aching muscles from too much activity.

9. Sage. *Latin name: Salvia officinalis* and Desert Sage, *Salvia apiana*

Sage is one of the Four Sacred Medicines that the Creator is said to have given to the First Nation Peoples. Tobacco was the first herb given, followed by sage, cedar, and sweetgrass for use in ceremonies, flavoring for food, and medicine. Sage is often used in sweat lodges and healing rituals, where the smell of this herb, when burned, adds an associated scent to the mystery and the event. It is also used as a medicine, tincture, herb-infused oil, and eaten fresh. The current use of sage in ceremonies is as protection against unwanted spirits, and the herb is believed to allow the individual to be protected from them.

What to use sage for

Cooking: Fresh and dried sage is used in many dishes, adding a delicious flavor to slow-cooked winter casseroles and soups. During the holidays, sage is a commonly used ingredient in stuffing for poultry.

Making herb oil: Mixing sage with olive oil or another oil of your choice adds a subtle flavor, which you can use in salad dressings or general cooking. After heavy exercise, it can be used as a massage oil to soothe aches and muscle pain.

Sore throat: Make a sage infusion and let it go cold. Use this for gargling when you have a sore throat. Also, it will provide antiseptic relief for tired voices if used twice a day.

Mouth ulcers: Use a cotton swab to apply a few drops of sage tincture to a mouth ulcer. The sage often soothes the short-term soreness. Remember, mouth ulcers usually present when the body is run down or lacks certain nutrients, so it may also need rest.

Menopausal symptoms: A capsule form of sage is readily available commercially and is said to improve the uncomfortable experiences of hot flashes, night sweats, and broken sleep commonly suffered during menopause.

What part of the plant do I collect?

Leaves to dry and process. To make a tincture, see PART 7.

When do I collect sage?

Sage is a perennial herb that tolerates frost and cold, so it is not required to be indoors in winter. Therefore, you can pick them all year round. However, there is a belief that sage varies in potency as a healing herb at different times of the year, so if used for cooking, collect leaves only when you require them.

To capture the more potent medical qualities of sage oil or sage for healing ceremonies, it is probably best to pick quantities of sage branches from spring to summer when the herb is actively growing. These can be dried until needed later in the year. To dry your herbs, see PART 7.

How do I store sage?

Sage leaves and branches can be cut from May to September for drying. Hang them upside down in a shady place out of direct reach of sunlight. Do not hang too close to lavender, or the scents will intermingle!

How to grow sage

If growing sage in a garden, be warned that not many plants can grow close to it. The roots of the sage plant exude a substance that deters other plants from germinating. However, strawberries and borage grow well beside sage in an herb garden. Sage also expands to quite a large shrub, and its flower stalks attract pollinators, butterflies, and ladybugs to feast on pollen and the insects that live on it. This herb requires a lot of space, healthy soil to start, and a good sunny spot, and it will live happily for years. Add a layer of mulch, compost, or leaf mold in the spring each year to provide nutrition for the herb. If it is close to strawberries, you can also give your sage plant a treat when you add ash and manure for them.

NOTES: Sage tea is commonly suggested as an aid to slow or stop the production of breast milk, though there seems to be no noted Native American usage of the herb for this purpose.

10. Sumac. *Latin Name: Rhus genus or Anacardiaceae family*

Sumac is a shrub that flowers in the wild with enormous spikes of pink blooms known as drupes. It's used to make the pink spice used to flavor many dishes worldwide. The Native American use of sumac included making pipes with the stem, various medicinal remedies, and adding flavor to tobacco mixtures.

What to use sumac for

Cooking: The drupes are best when ground into a pink spice and added to salads and meat dishes, imparting its lemony flavor to any dish.

High blood pressure: Consumption of sumac is known to decrease high blood pressure, so this is a valuable herb for anyone with this condition. The flavonoids and polyphenols it contains may also help keep cholesterol in the blood at reasonable levels.

Sore throats: Use the drupes to make a soothing sumac lemonade, also known as rhus juice, Indian lemonade, and sumac-ade. Pick a handful of drupes and squeeze them slightly to release their goodness into the water for a refreshing drink. Take care not to squeeze or pierce the berries too much because there are tiny hairs in sumac fruit that can be irritating if swallowed. Leave the berries overnight in water, and then strain the resulting liquid through fine muslin to remove the tiny hairs of the drupes. Discard the berries, and drink the pink sumac lemonade the next day. You can always add honey to sweeten the juice if you like. This pink liquid will be a hit with younger members of the family! A sumac beverage also helps if you have a fever.

Smoking mixtures: The drupes are used by Native Americans with tobacco in smoking mixtures. They used the stems of sumac for pipes because they have a soft center removed easily. Sumac pipes were very popular with tribes in the northern states.

Tanning: Traditionally, sumac leaves and bark add color to fabric and leather. Powdered sumac can stain when the powder is mixed with water. It becomes evident when you use it in food, and the dish acquires a pink coloring.

What part of the plant do I collect?

When harvesting sumac, collect the flowering heads (drupes). Drupes are used for sumac lemonade. They are also used dry and make a pink spice with a lemony flavor that you can add to cooked dishes.

When do I collect sumac?

It is recommended to pick most herbs and berries in the morning on a sunny day. With sumac, the drupes are ripe in the fall, so pick them, scrutinize them for insect damage, and discard any imperfect ones.

A word of warning: There are some poisonous forms of sumac. They are the ones with white flowers. So check the plant label carefully if buying from a garden center, and be especially careful if collecting in the wild. Only pick pink drupes!

How do I store sumac?

To store sumac, pick the ripe drupes and immediately use them as a fresh ingredient. Or, if you prefer, extend their flavor and dry them indoors out of direct sunlight.

A garden shed area is perfect for storing them! Tie them in bunches and hang them upside down. When the herbs are dry, you can grind them in a food processor to make the scarlet-pink spice used in many winter recipes.

How to grow sumac

Sumac can grow as tall as 15 feet (4.57 m), so make sure you have room for it in your garden. It is possible to cultivate sumac in a pot, but it will be much smaller. Although sumac enjoys a sunny location, they are not fussy about the soil. Still, if available, they will benefit from some organic content like leaf mold, compost, or manure. In the first year of growth, check for soil dryness often. Ensure you water it in arid summers. After that, the rainfall will do the job. However, keep an eye on sumac in a pot as it can dry out.

You will need to prune your sumac plant every year. However, try incorporating your drupe picking in the fall with pruning, and you can enjoy the pink flowers for many years.

Another feature of growing sumac is that this plant spreads by rhizome (root) and will try to spread yearly. The rhizomes are quite spiky when cut, so you should try to cut them before they become too large. You can repot as a gift rather than have spiky roots showing up in your garden.

11. Yarrow. *Latin name: Achillea millefolium*

Yarrow has delightful silvery leaves and brightly colored flowers that bees adore, so planting yarrow in your garden will bring wildlife and color and add to your natural herb remedies available for picking.

What to use yarrow for

Acne: The Cherokee use of yarrow water for acne is something Jacob remembers his grandmother making for his older cousin. Use some hot water on the leaves and let them cool. Then apply the liquid using cotton swabs onto the affected area.

Colds: Yarrow leaves contain anti-inflammatory chemicals used in yarrow tea, which can help keep colds at bay. Just take some leaves, add hot water, and strain the leaves away before drinking.

Salads: You can also eat leaves directly from the plant or add them to salads for a tasty different addition to your usual greens.

Improve circulation: Yarrow leaves were used to boost circulation in traditional Native American medicine. Nibbling on a few leaves as you pass by is good!

Toothache: Said to soothe toothache in Cherokee knowledge. Place the chewed leaves in your mouth close to the affected area. You can apply yarrow oil if you make some oil infused with leaves.

Insect repellent: The leaves are insecticidal, so add some yarrow stems with leaves to drawers to keep insects away from your clothes. Historically, in Europe, yarrow was hung over doorways and was said to keep illness outside the home.

Nosebleeds: Yarrow is helpful for frequent nosebleeds. Drink a tea made from yarrow daily.

A word of warning: There are mixed reviews on its use if you are pregnant or breastfeeding, so do not use without seeking advice from your herbalist and doctor.

What part of the plant do I collect?

Leaves must be dried and stored out of direct sunlight for use when the plant is not in season. Fresh leaves can be eaten, added to salads, and used to make yarrow oil.

How do I store yarrow?

Hang stems of yarrow leaves upside down and allow the plant to dry. Feel the leaves, and once dry, store them in a glass herb jar, ensuring they are placed out of direct sunlight. Make a label from some old paper to label it.

How to grow yarrow

Yarrow can be grown from seed indoors and is well worth it for the beautiful colors it brings to your garden. Flowers vary from white to bright pink and are adored by bees and other pollinators. Plant the seeds indoors in April in a pot. However, you may need to cover the pot with polythene to maintain heat and moisture. Once they have germinated, they are big enough, and when all danger of frost is over, place them in the ground in a sunny place with some space to expand. They will reach a height of about a foot and spread sideways, so they are perfect in the middle of a flower bed with smaller flowers in front of them. Save the seeds from the flower heads each year by shaking them into a paper envelope and replanting them the following year.

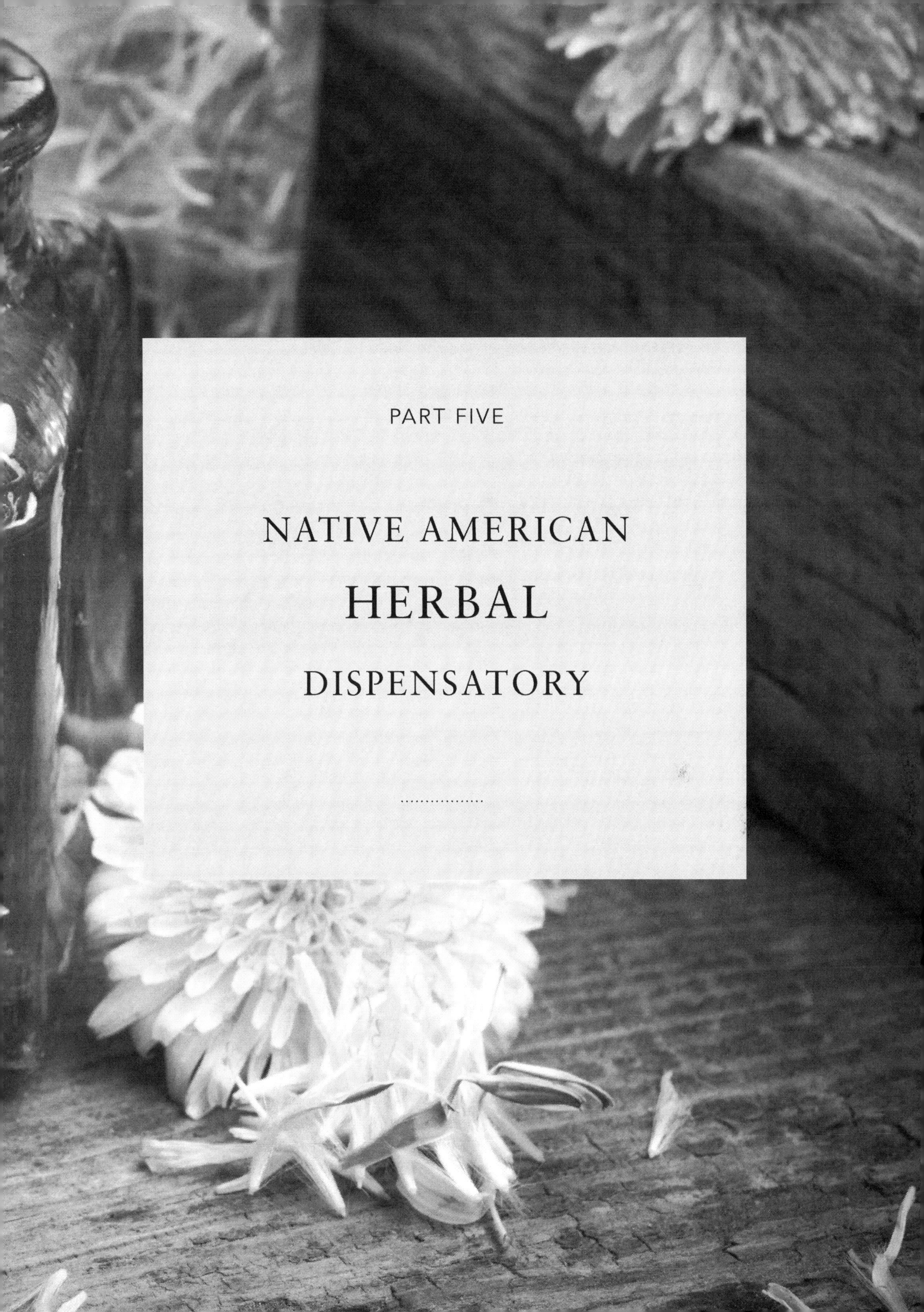

PART FIVE

NATIVE AMERICAN HERBAL DISPENSATORY

Your comprehensive guide to medicinal plants used by Native Americans

HOW TO USE THIS SECTION

There is a detailed list of eleven widely used herbs in PART 4. But here, Jacob presents the rest of his top 101 preferred plants and herbs found in the US. Everything is listed by ailment, which part of the herb to use, its preparation, and what to avoid. If looking for a particular plant, then search for it by name alphabetically. The list includes the Latin name in brackets for easy identification.

If you are searching for an ailment, a condition, or an illness and want to find which plant you can use, then search for the condition's name alphabetically in PART 6. Plants are suggested there, which you can read about in detail in PART 4 or PART 5.

Herbs to avoid if pregnant: If you are pregnant, nursing, or thinking of starting a family, a list of plants to avoid is located at the end of PART 5.

NOTES are referencing official herbal reports and national pharmacopeia:
German Federal Health Agency's Commission E was established in 1978 to independently review and evaluate scientific literature and case studies on herb and plant medications worldwide.
US Pharmacopeia, British Pharmacopeia, The Botanical Safety Handbook, AHPA

Jacob's Complete List of Herbs

1. Aloe Vera *(Aloe barbadensis)*
2. Angelica *(Angelica archangelica)*
3. Arnica *(Arnica montana)*
   Bearberry - see Uva Ursi (85)
   Bear Root - see Osha (61)
4. Blackberry - see PART 4
5. Black Cohosh *(Actaea racemosa)*
6. Black Haw *(Viburnum prunifolium)*
7. Blue Cohosh *(Caulophyllum thalictroides)*
8. Boneset *(Eupatorium perfoliatum)*
9. Borage *(Borago officinalis)*
10. Boswellia *(Boswellia serrata)*
11. Broom Snakeweed *(Gutierrezia sarothrae)*
12. Buckbrush - see PART 4
13. Buffaloberry *(Shepherdia argentea)*
14. Burdock *(Arctium lappa)*
15. California Poppy *(Eschscholzia californica)*
16. Cat's Claw *(Uncaria tomentosa)*
17. Cattail - see PART 4
18. Cedar *(Cedrus)*
19. Centaury *(Centaurium erythraea)*
20. Chamomile *(Matricaria recutita)*
21. Chasteberry *(Vitex agnus-castus)*
22. Chickweed *(Stellaria media)*
23. Chokeberry *(Aronia melanocarpa)*
    Chokecherry - see Wild Black Cherry (89)
24. Cleavers *(Galium aparine)*
25. Coltsfoot *(Tussilago farfara)*
26. Comfrey *(Symphytum officinale)*
    Cramp Bark - see Black Haw (6)
27. Damiana *(Turnera diffusa)*
28. Dandelion - see PART 4
29. Devil's Claw *(Harpagophytum procumbens)*
30. Dogwood *(Cornus florida)*
31. Echinacea *(Echinacea angustifolia)*
32. Elderflower - see PART 4

33. Evening Primrose *(Oenothera biennis)*
34. (American) Feverfew *(Parthenium integrifolium)*
35. Feverfew *(Tanacetum parthenium)*
36. Feverwort *(Triosteum perfoliatum)*
37. Flaxseed - see PART 4
38. Garlic *(Allium sativum)* and Wild Garlic *(Allium tricoccum)*
39. Gentiana *(Gentiana andrewsii)*
    Ginger - see Wild Ginger (91)
40. (American) Ginseng *(Panax quinquefolius)*
41. Goldenrod *(Solidago spp.)*
42. Goldenseal *(Hydrastis canadensis)*
43. Gravel Root / Joe Pye Weed *(Eupatorium purpureum)*
44. Hawthorn *(Crataegus spp.)*
45. Hemlock: Western Hemlock *(Tsuga heterophyla)* and Eastern Hemlock *(Tsuga canadensis)*
46. Honeysuckle *(Lonicera sempervirens, ciliosa, and hispidula)*
47. Hops *(Humulus lupulus)*
48. Horsemint (*Monarda punctata)*
49. Horsetail *(Equisetum arvense)*
50. Juniper *(Juniperus communis)*
51. (Desert) Lavender *(Condea emoryi)*
52. Lemon Balm (*Melissa officinalis)*
53. Mesquite *(Prosopis glandulosa)*
54. Milkweed *(Asclepias spp.)*
55. Mint - see PART 4
56. Mullein *(Verbascum thapsus)*
57. Nettle *(Urtica dioica)*
58. Oak *(Quercus rubra)*
59. Oats *(Avena sativa)* and Wild Oats *(Chasmanthium latifolium)*
60. Oregon Grape (*Mahonia aquifolium)*
61. Osha *(Ligusticum porteri)*
62. Passionflower *(Passiflora)*
    Peppermint - see Mint (55)
63. Pinon / Pinyon Pine *(Pinus edulis)*
64. (White) Pine *(Pinus strobus)*
65. Plantain *(Plantago major)*
66. Poke Root (*Phytolacca decandra, Phytolacca americana)*
67. Prickly Pear Cactus *(Opuntia engelmannii)*
68. Rabbit Tobacco *(Pseudognaphalium obtusifolium)*
69. Red Clover *(Trifolium pratense)*
    Rosehip - see Wild Rose (93)
70. Rosemary - see PART 4
71. Sage - see PART 4
72. Saltbush *(Atriplex canescens)*
73. Sarsaparilla *(Smilax regelii, Smilax aspera)*
74. Sassafras *(Sassafras albidum)*
75. Saw Palmetto *(Serenoa repens)*
76. Seneca Snakeroot *(Polygala senega)*
    Shavegrass - see Horsetail (49)
77. Skullcap *(Scutellaria lateriflora)*
78. Slippery Elm *(Ulmus rubra)*
79. St. John's Wort *(Hypericum perforatum)*
80. Stoneseed *(Lithospermum)*
81. Sumac - see PART 4
82. Sweetgrass *(Hierochloe odorata)*
83. Thyme *(Thymus vulgaris)*
84. Tobacco *(Nicotiana)*
85. Uva Ursi *(Arctostaphylos)*
86. Valerian *(Valeriana officinalis, Valeriana edulis)*
87. Western Skunk Cabbage *(Lysichiton americanus)*
88. White Willow *(Salix alba)*
89. Wild Black Cherry *(Prunus serotina)*
90. Wild Carrot *(Daucus carota)*
91. Wild Ginger *(Asarum canadense)*
92. Wild Lettuce *(Lactuca virosa)*
    Wild Mountain Thyme *(Thymus serpyllum)* see Thyme (83)
93. Wild Rose *(Rosa acicularis)*
94. Wild Yam *(Dioscorea villosa)*
95. Witch Hazel *(Hamamelis virginiana)*
96. Wormwood *(Artemisia campestris)*
97. Yarrow - see PART 4
98. Yellow Dock *(Rumex crispus)*
99. Yerba Santa / Mountain Balm *(Eriodictyon californicum)*
100. Yew *(Taxus brevifolia, Taxus canadensis)*
101. Yucca *(Yucca elata Engelmann)*

JACOB'S COMPLETE LIST OF HERBS AND HOW TO UTILIZE THEM

1. Aloe Vera
(Aloe barbadensis)

Aloe vera was artistically painted on the walls of Egyptian tombs, where it represented a gift for the funeral rites of a deceased Pharaoh. It was known as the "immortality plant." The Greeks used it as a plant that could slow down hair loss, and today, this succulent is a houseplant all over the world. It enjoys sunny, warm conditions in the wild, where there is no danger of frost. It thrives in the southern US, Mexico, and in climates like Barbados, which gives the plant its Latin name. Native American use included topical use of the gel to aid in healing wounds, cuts, and burns, including sunburn. It was referred to as the medicine plant, burn plant, and mystery plant and was seen as a gift from the Creator. Aloe gel, obtained by cutting fresh leaves, was used to reduce inflammation, speed healing of cuts, and act as an analgesic and antimicrobial. Modern research tests the use of aloe, administered orally, to aid with pain from arthritis.

What ailments it helps
Arthritis
Burns
Constipation
Cuts
Hair loss
Inflammation
Lower blood sugar
Lower potassium
Ringworm
Stomach ulcers
Sunburn
Wound healing

Which part to use
Leaves

How to consume it
The correct way to use the plant is to cut a leaf section, trim the side edges, and remove the clear gel from the inside.

Gel: Use a freshly cut leaf; open it and use the clear internal gel for wound and burn care. Use in a compress, or create an ointment – see PART 7. Never drink the gel.

First aid: It is an excellent emergency first aid kit for wound care and burns due to its analgesic and anti-inflammatory action. Use the gel directly.

Constipation: Aloe is approved for this use by Commission E in Germany.

Arthritis: Tests are taking place using aloe juice taken orally to aid pain, which may lower blood sugar and potassium levels, according to recent studies.

Hair loss: A traditional use in Greece, applied externally.

Juice: Germany's Commission E approved the juice of the leaves taken orally as a laxative. Juice is made from leaves (usually bought commercially). Jacob recommends you purchase organic aloe vera juice with no additives or preservatives, as it is just too difficult to make yourself. Taking two to three ounces of juice each day should be enough, and you can add a teaspoon of honey and some water if you don't like the taste. It is said to lower blood sugar and potassium. Taken this way, it may also help with pain from arthritis and the various ailments listed.

2. Angelica
(Angelica archangelica)

Since all parts of this plant are edible, the candied stem and root have been added to cake decorations for centuries. This herb may taste strangely familiar if you have ever tasted gin or Chartreuse, the French liqueur, as it is also added to them. Known as dong quai in China, the root has been used for a thousand years for sinus congestion, anemia, allergies, headaches, PMS, and to improve circulation. It may also reduce pain, relax uterine muscles, and treat weakness after childbirth. Native Americans used all parts of the angelica plant. From seed to root, all parts are edible, and its unique flavor is slightly sweet with a hint of bitterness and licorice.

What ailments it helps
Allergies
Anemia
Bronchitis
Childbirth problems
Coughs
Fluid retention
Headaches
Indigestion
Liver and bile disorders
Loss of appetite
Pleurisy
PMS
Poor circulation
Sinus congestion
Sore muscles

Which parts to use
Fruit, leaves, seeds, stems, and roots

How to consume it
Roots: Dig some seeds in the fall and clean, cut, and grate into smaller pieces, and dry or freeze them for the colder months. Harvest the young leaves during the first year of growth.

Seeds: An ointment from the seeds is used to treat body lice.

Leaves and whole herb: Leaves are used as a diuretic. Pick fresh leaves if you can, or dry some leaves for winter.

Leaf infusion: Add a teaspoon of leaves to boiling water and strain before drinking as a diuretic. The aniseed flavor will encourage frequent trips and clear out your system.

Roots: Roots are used to make cough and bronchitis syrup and tinctures.

Carefully dig up a small section of root, clean it, and then use two tablespoons of the fresh root, cut or grated into small pieces. See the syrup and tincture recipes in PART 7.

Root infusion: Grate two teaspoons of the root in water and bring it to a boil. Let it simmer for 15 minutes, strain the liquid into a sterilized container, and drink it hot or cold.

Root oil: Add fresh or dried root to oil in a sealed jar, place it in a dry, dark space, and shake daily for 4-6 weeks. Then strain the solids, return the infused oil to the sealed jars, and return to storage for 4-6 months. Angelica oil is pleasantly soothing for sore muscles. See the plant oil recipe in PART 7.

NOTES: Sometimes the oil can cause skin irritation, so use it in small quantities.

WARNING: There have been suggestions that angelica (taken orally) may increase the chance of uterine contractions, so best to avoid if pregnant.

3. Arnica
(Arnica montana)

Although the plant is toxic if ingested orally, Native Americans and Europeans have used this plant for centuries as a healing ointment to reduce inflammation, treat bruises and sprains, and soothe muscle aches. Only use externally.

What ailments it helps
Bruises
Inflammation
Pain relief
Rheumatism
Sore muscles
Sprains

Which parts to use
Flowers, leaves, and roots

The flowers are added to herb oil and used as an ointment. In addition, the flowers are also dried for edible and decorative use.

Cut leaves before the plant flowers and use dried in oil for winter. See recipes for ointments and oils in PART 7.

The root and its rhizome are washed, dried, and sometimes ground into powder or added to ointments.

How to consume it
Arnica is said to heal any bruise as an ointment, provided there is no open wound or bleeding. Apply directly to the bruise or aching area externally. Do not apply to an open wound with blood.

WARNING: Arnica is poisonous in large quantities. Do not ingest.

Michael Moore advises against its use, even topically, if pregnant.

Bearberry - see Uva Ursi (85)

Bear Root - see Osha (61)

4. Blackberry - *see PART 4*

5. Black Cohosh
(Actaea racemosa)

The word cohosh is said to be the Algonquian word for pregnancy, and its use is focused on women. This herb is native to Canada and eastern America and grows wild in woodlands. Its extensive use by Native Americans provided newly-arrived settlers their knowledge from practical, observed use. It is full of nutrients and contains no caffeine. Cohosh is beneficial for female health problems and contains phytoestrogen (similar to estrogen).

What ailments it helps
Aches
Menopausal symptoms
Menstruation cramps
Pain relief
PMS
Tinnitus
To bring on labor (39 weeks+)

Which part to use
Roots

How to consume it
Tea: The black cohosh roots are used in teas to ease aches and pains.

Tea infusion: Dig up a portion of the root, which can be dried and grated to use in a tea infusion. Using a medium-sized fresh root, chop and boil with 1 cup (0.24 l) of water for 3 minutes, then strain it. Add honey or ginger for flavor.

WARNING: Do not use black cohosh if you have hepatitis (viral) or if you are pregnant.

Only use under medical supervision during the last week of pregnancy.

6. Black Haw
(Viburnum prunifolium)

Also known as cramp bark in Europe, its close cousin is the guelder rose. The edible pink berries are also called European cranberry and are still used in Canada as a cranberry substitute in making jam, juice, and teas. However, unripe fruit may cause stomach upsets, so it is best eaten cooked.

Native American Cherokee and Delaware tribes used the herb as an antispasmodic for the female reproductive system (i.e., dysmenorrhea - painful periods). As a nerve sedative, it is included in the UK's National Formulary as a fluid extract, compound tincture, and compound elixir for nerve sedative and antispasmodic in asthma, hysteria, and tetanus (lockjaw).

What ailments it helps
Gynecological problems
Heart palpitations
Lowers blood pressure
Rheumatism
Sedative

Which part to use
Berries

How to consume it
Tincture: Use a tincture of the bark in alcohol, add drops in a glass of water, and use daily, as recommended by a qualified herbalist. To make your tinctures, see PART 7.

7. Blue Cohosh
(Caulophyllum thalictroides)

This plant is also known as papoose root, and is not related to the black cohosh plant. Many Native American tribes used blue cohosh to help with childbirth. It is also used to regulate menstrual disorders. The Meskwaki used it to treat genitourinary issues, and the Omaha made blue cohosh tea to bring down a fever. In other parts of the world, blue cohosh is used as a diuretic and an expectorant for chest coughs.

What ailments it helps
Childbirth problems
Contraction-type spasms
Coughs
Diuretic
Fevers
Fluid retention
Gynecological issues (e.g., amenorrhea - lack of periods, dysmenorrhea - painful periods)
Rheumatic symptoms
To bring on labor (39 weeks+)

Which part to use
Roots

How to consume it
Root: Dig up and dry the root, then grate into tiny pieces for use in tea or powder form.

Tea: Use grated root powder in an infusion, strain the liquid, and sip for painful periods or to suppress heavy bleeding. See the recipe for black cohosh tea.

Traditionally, this was also useful in the last week of pregnancy, as it was said to lead to pain-free labor. However, great caution is needed in pregnancy because the root is also known to cause abortions if taken early in pregnancy. Therefore, it is highly recommended to consult a medical professional before use.

As a tincture/herb oil - see PART 7.

NOTES: Leaves and seeds are poisonous.

WARNING: Only use under medical supervision during the last week of pregnancy.

8. Boneset
(Eupatorium perfoliatum)

Settlers watched how Native Americans used this plant. They took boneset leaves and flowers in infusions and decoctions to help bring down high fevers. The Cherokee used leaves and plant infusions to increase sweating and cool the body. When influenza was incredibly painful, an infusion of the leaves helped to relieve pain and ease the headaches that arrived with the flu. Leaves were also picked and applied as a poultice to ease rheumatic pain at the sore spot. It is possible to make an ointment oil to use similarly today. The Iroquois made a root decoction taken orally to treat alcoholism. As boneset has a very bitter taste, when settlers used it to treat malaria, they added molasses to make it sweeter on the palate. An infusion of boneset, comfrey, and nettle is said to help heal broken bones.

Which ailments it helps
Bone healer
Fever reducer
Flu symptoms
Muscle and body aches
Pain relief
Rheumatism

Which parts to use
Leaves, flowers, and roots

How to consume it
Tea: Prepare leaf infusions in boiling water, then strain. Add honey to make it more palatable.

Leaves: Pick leaves, dry them, and make them into powder, which can be applied directly onto aching joints or muscles to bring relief – see PART 7.

Tincture: Make your own by adding leaves to alcohol – see PART 7.

WARNING: Avoid if nursing or pregnant.

9. Borage
(Borago officinalis)

Borage is often a companion of strawberry plants and has an elegant, blue edible flower that adds color to summer cocktails. In Europe, borage was infused in tea and given to those convalescing after a long illness. It's a tonic for the heart and blood. There is less use of this herb internally since a study found that if taken in excess regularly, the alkaloids contained in the leaves may build up in the liver. It is safe in small amounts, so use borage sparingly. Eat the flowers in salads and use the ointment externally. In the past, borage was used to relieve diarrhea. It has long been used for urinary conditions (bladder and kidney problems).

Which ailments it helps

Bladder and kidney problems
Boils
Bruising
Coughs
Diarrhea
Eczema
Indigestion
Insect bites and stings
Rashes
Sore throats

Which parts to use

Leaves, flowers, and seeds

How to consume it

Tea: A tea from the flowers and leaves is a good cough and sore throat soother. Use 2 teaspoons of fresh or 1 teaspoon of dried leaves in boiling water and strain before drinking.

Skin conditions: Borage contains essential oils used externally on insect bites and stings, reducing swelling and bruising.

Poultice: Make a poultice from fresh leaves for insect bites and stings and apply it directly. Traditionally, it's bound with dried raffia or similar material, but you can use gauze or a bandage.

Ointment: Use dried leaves in winter for powder. Pick and hang them upside down out of the sunlight to dry them. Then, use the ointment oil made from dried leaf powder directly on the affected areas.

Rashes and eczema: Ointment oil can also be made from pressed seeds. Rich in unsaturated fatty acids, the oil from the seeds relieves eczema, rashes, and nourishes sensitive skin. However, the process is tricky, so Jacob suggests buying oil from health food stores.

NOTES: When taking it internally, use it occasionally, not every day. This is vital because borage contains alkaloids that can build up in the liver over time.

10. Boswellia
(Boswellia serrata)

This tree is also called frankincense, one of the gifts offered to Jesus in his manger, a gift from the Three Wise Men from the East. As well as medicinally, the resin from this tree is used commercially in paint and varnish, while its scent in toiletries, perfumes, and incense is a worldwide custom. Ceremonially, many Native American people have burned this plant to produce a fragrant smoke that will please the nose and the Creator.

What ailments it helps

Asthma
Inflammation
Jaundice
Osteoarthritis
Rheumatoid arthritis
Thyroid function
To suppress cancer cell reproduction

Which part to use

After cutting the tree's bark to produce resin, harvest it through the summer and autumn, repeating the process for three years in a row. Then, for the next three years, allow the trees to rest before gathering in March or April of the next term; three years harvest and three years rest.

How to consume it

Jacob recommends purchasing the resin or essential oil to create your tincture or ointment to ease the above ailments or purchase supplements. Always buy organic if at all possible.

To make your tincture or ointment, please see PART 7.

WARNING: Avoid if nursing or pregnant.

11. Broom Snakeweed
(Gutierrezia sarothrae)

This yellow-colored spike of flowers grows wild, and its use by several Native American tribes is well documented. For example, the Blackfoot used flowers in steam therapy. The Dakota used flowers for horses as a laxative. The Lakota used a decoction for colds, coughs, and dizziness, and the Navajo chewed leaves and applied them to wounds, stings, and snakebites. In addition, they used ashes on their bodies to relieve headaches and dizziness.

What ailments it helps
Colds
Coughs
Dizziness
Fevers
Headaches
Insect bites and stings
Respiratory congestion
Snakebites
Wound healing

Which parts to use
Flowers, leaves, and roots

How to consume it
Steam therapy: Use the flowers and throw them onto heated stones or fires to make scented steam to relieve nasal congestion.

Use the ashes from steam therapy: Keep them and follow the Native American custom to use them for headaches by applying a little on the skin, provided that the timber used in burning has not been chemically treated. Wash off carefully after use, and do not place it near the eyes. Also, ensure that it is not applied to children's skin.

Decoction: Use the leaves and roots and make a decoction as a remedy for colds and coughs – see PART 7.

Poultice: Broom snakeweed leaves are also used as a poultice for stings and wound healing – see PART 7.

12. Buckbrush
see PART 4

13. Buffaloberry
(Shepherdia argentea)

Native to the Great Plains States in the US, three species of buffaloberry were eaten as a fruit and used as medicine. It's also known as silverleaf due to the color of its foliage.

What ailments it helps
Acne
Arthritis
Boils
Cuts
Gallstones
Insect bites
Sore eyes
Swelling
Wound healing

Which parts to use
Berries, bark, leaves, and stems

How to consume it
Food: Pick the berries, eat them fresh, and use them in cooking. They make splendid homemade jellies and desserts. It was traditionally made into "Indian ice-cream" dessert for special occasions. The berries provide vitamin C and are rich in carotenoid and phenolic antioxidant compounds, including lycopene. However, the berries also contain saponins, which may cause indigestion. The juice of the berries are said to help gallstones.

Ointment: To reduce swelling, skin conditions, and for pain, squeeze the juice of the berries and use in an anti-inflammatory ointment - see PART 7.

An infusion of the bark was used to bathe sore eyes.

A decoction of the leaves and stems was used to create a wash for sores, bites, cuts, etc.

The buffaloberry is often used to make fabric dye and shampoo.

NOTES: The fruit contains low concentrations of saponins. Even though they are toxic, these substances are very poorly absorbed by the body and so tend to pass through without causing harm. Therefore, do not consume large quantities.

14. Burdock
(Arctium lappa)

This plant has many edible parts: the leaves, stems, and roots, though stems and roots need to be cooked first with several water changes to remove toxins. Besides being a food source, the Chippewa used burdock as a cough soother and to relieve congestion. The leaves are also thick enough to be sewn together for use as headbands to offer some shade from summer sunshine. Greater burdock is also seen in the US but is smaller than its European cousin.

What ailments it helps
Acne
Coughs
Diaphoretic (aids sweating)
Eczema
Gallbladder health
Gout
Hair loss
Psoriasis
Skin ulcers

Which parts to use
Roots, leaves, and stems

How to consume it
Cough syrup: Dry the roots of burdock and dandelion to make a cough syrup. Together they can be grated and powdered to add to your mixture easily. Add extra flavor (such as cinnamon sticks or cassia bark) if you like. Add sugar to sweeten and thicken the mix – see PART 7.

Root oil: For hair and scalp, root oil extract promotes hair growth.

Infusion or ointment: Use fresh or dried root to create an infusion, let it go cold, then you have a wash for acne, skin ulcers, or sores. Dried root can be added to an ointment for applying to skin conditions – see PART 7.

Food: The leaves can be eaten fresh and the stems cooked. However, roots and stems need some care when preparing. Make sure you change the water, reheat the mixture again, and discard this water, too. This method removes or reduces any toxins left in the herb mixture.

Clothing: The leaves were woven together and used to make sustainable head coverings to shade from the hot sun and are sometimes held in place by attaching a strip of tree bark.

WARNING: Avoid if nursing, pregnant, or trying to become pregnant.

15. California Poppy
(Eschscholzia californica)

The California poppy is a colorful addition to any flower garden and has many medicinal uses for Native American people. Its sedative qualities make it very useful for treating young children, and it provides relief from toothaches and headaches. It is reported that its sap is also an effective treatment for head lice.

What ailments it helps
Headache
Hyperactivity in young children
Lice treatment
Pain relief
Sedative
Spasm relaxant
Toothache

Which part to use
The whole plant is harvested and dried or processed. It is best to wait until the flowers arrive before harvesting.

How to consume it
Sap (from stem and flower) can be used directly on a painful area of the skin or mouth. When applied to the scalp, it's also an effective treatment for head lice.

Dried flowers infused in boiling water are a natural treatment for hyperactive children. In addition, it is a mild sedative for young babies and children.

A tincture can be made with the dried plant and then used by taking drops in water to relieve pain and other symptoms.

NOTES: Always check with your herbalist before giving any herbal remedies to children.

WARNING: Avoid if nursing or pregnant.

16. Cat's Claw
(Uncaria tomentosa)

Not native to the US, it is classified as invasive in Florida due to the ease of spreading. The underground tubers and the spiked thorns, from which it gets its name, and the vines curl around anything they can climb. Its bright yellow flowers can be seen as a yellow carpet on many streets. Although it is used extensively by the Andean people, its use by Native Americans is less well-known but is frequently used in their infusions.

What ailments it helps
Arthritis
Fatigue
Immune system disorders
Lyme disease
Pancreatic problems
Rheumatism

Which part to use
The bark of the tree or shrub.

How to consume it
Anti-inflammatory: Helps rheumatic and arthritic disorders when used as ointment topically. The liquid extract or tincture can be taken as a health tonic.

Immune system booster: Recent studies show that diseases that affect the body's immune system (AIDS, PMS, chronic fatigue syndrome) may be helped by using this herb. Oxindole alkaloids found in cat's claw have been shown to stimulate the immune system.

Cat's claw is a treatment for Lyme disease.

Make a tincture: Use the bark to make a tincture – see PART 7.

Ensure to consume adequate water daily, especially when using this herb.

WARNING: Avoid if nursing or pregnant.

17. Cattail
see PART 4

18. Cedar

(Cedrus)

Native Americans utilized everything the cedar tree had to offer, from using the wood to make arrows and spears to burning it as incense and fuel. Members of the tribes sacrificed it to the sacred fire during sweat lodge ceremonies. Great hollowed-out logs of red cedar were used to make their giant canoes up to 60 feet (18.29 m) in length. It was the mainstay of home-building, using cedar planks. In addition, it was used in the ever-impressive cultural artwork, such as enormous totem poles and detailed carved masks.

Wood, bark, leaves, and oil have all been used by Native Americans as medicine. In addition, cedar is used worldwide for its disinfectant and antiseptic qualities. Also, the oil can be used around the home as an insect repellent.

What ailments it helps

Acne
Asthma
Bronchial infections
Flatulence
Improve appetite and digestion
Joint pain relief
Respiratory issues
Skin irritations
Warts
Wound healing

Which parts to use

Wood, bark, branches, leaves, and oil

How to consume it

Tea: Simmer 2 cups (0.47 l) of fresh chopped cedar branches in 4 cups (0.95 l) of boiling water for about 10 minutes. Strain off the cedar and sweeten with maple syrup to taste.

Salves and oils – see PART 7. Jacob advises that commercially produced oil may be an easier option, from which ointment or salve can be made and applied to sore joints or for skin irritations.

Decoction – see PART 7.

WARNING: Avoid if pregnant.

19. Centaury

(Centaurium erythraea)

Although now common in the US, this plant is originally native to Europe. Centaury is used worldwide. The Council of Europe lists centaury as a natural food flavoring. In the US, centaury can be utilized in beverages up to a strength of 0.0002%-0.0008%. Germany's Commission E also approves it for loss of appetite and dyspeptic complaints.

The German Commission E approves 1 to 2 g of herb daily, while other uses for dyspepsia specify as much as 6 g per day.

Traditionally, it was used to increase psychic power by witches and is a patron herb of herbalists, who used it to "repel anger."
Pick the flowers, leaves, and stems of the aerial plant from late June to mid-July or when the flowers arrive. When you first pick this herb, its pungent odor slowly disappears as it dries. Dry the herb for winter use by hanging it in a shady area. When completely dry, make a powder or infusion. Do not use the roots.

Native American use of this herb includes the following:

What ailments it helps
Heartburn
Indigestion
Muscle pains
Stimulates appetite

Which parts to use
Flowers, leaves, and stems, not the roots.

How to consume it
The dried herb can be given as an infusion half an hour before meals (limit of 3-4 cups per day) to increase appetite or for indigestion, or as a tonic for those who feel run down. When ground into powder, drink this infusion to ease pain in sore muscles or joints.

20. Chamomile
(Matricaria recutita)

Chamomile is the world's favorite herbal tea for relaxation and preparation for sleeping. It is the best seller around the world to cure insomnia naturally. For Native Americans, the medicinal uses of chamomile included an infusion to ease menstrual cramps or stomach pain. It is also reported to have been used as an aphrodisiac. In addition, the sedative qualities of the herbal flower tea are so gentle they can be given to young children, and the use of the herbal tea to soothe sore throats is also well-known.

What ailments it helps
Earache
Hay fever
Hemorrhoids
Inflammation
Insomnia
Menstrual cramps
Muscle spasms
Nausea
Neuralgia
Rheumatic pain
Sore throats
Toothache

Which part to use
Flowers

How to consume it
Flowers are dried for infusions or made into a tincture, essential oil, cosmetics, and ointment. It is used in aromatherapy and is often included in bath toiletries. You can purchase the essential oil, or you can make your own. Optimum chamomile extracts contain about 50 percent alcohol.

Tea and infusion: Oral infusion of chamomile tea is prepared from dried flowers. It is recommended as a tea by Commission E in Germany. It is suitable for use with children and adults, as it is a natural product. It acts as a natural antihistamine.

Lotion: For external use, it soothes earache, toothache, and neuralgia.

Tea: Powder from dried flowers is added to tea bag mixtures.

Tinctures: Make a tincture using flowers steeped in alcohol, which extracts the medicinal ingredients. First, strain the mixture to remove the flowers. Next, store the fluid in a dropper bottle and take it mixed with some water. This can be used in the bath to soothe hemorrhoids. See PART 7 for more details on making a tincture.

21. Chasteberry
(Vitex agnus-castus)

This herb was supposed to help monks balance their hormone levels (to keep them chaste), thus the name. However, the berries of the chasteberry have been shown to help regulate hormone levels in females throughout their life cycle, whether PMS, endometriosis, or menopause symptoms. Eating berries also stimulates breast milk for nursing mothers, but this is not advised as the safety has not been adequately tested.

What ailments it helps
Acne or other skin conditions
Endometriosis
Fibroid prevention
Menopause symptoms
Painful breasts
PMS
Seizures

Which parts to use
Berries, leaves, and flowers

How to consume it
Infusion: Berries and flowers are used in teas. Flowers can be dried before they turn into berries.

Food: Berries can be eaten fresh. They can also be dried and ground into a powder and taken orally.

Essential oil: Leaves and flowers can be used to make essential oil. To make essential oil and tinctures, please see PART 7.

WARNING: Avoid if nursing or pregnant.

22.Chickweed
(Stellaria media)

So named because chickens love eating it if it grows in their feeding areas, chickweed is often regarded as a common weed. Humans also eat it fresh or dried for the flavonoids, vitamin C, and alkaloids it contains. However, for Native Americans, it was a plant to use for eye infections and to reduce inflammation in rheumatic conditions with stiffness in the joints.

What ailments it helps
Coughs
Eye infections
Gout
Inflammation

Joint stiffness
Rheumatism
Skin irritations
Sore throats
Wound healing

Which parts to use
Flowers, leaves, and stems

How to consume it
As a tea or chew, it eased rheumatism.

Food: It can be eaten fresh or dried as a food source. Fresh leaves can be lightly cooked, made into soup, or added raw to salads.

Infusion: The Cherokee dried the whole herb and made infusions with water, utilizing it as a soothing cough mixture or for sore, hoarse throats. The same liquid was used as an eye wash for infected eyes.

Poultice: For skin irritations and wounds, use the leaves to make a poultice, dry the leaves, make them into a powder, and use them as a wound healer. Shake the powder over the affected area and then use leaves as a poultice. It was also used as a poultice and lotion to calm skin conditions. Finally, add leaves or powder directly to bathwater to relieve inflammation.

WARNING: Avoid if nursing or pregnant.

23. Chokeberry
(Aronia melanocarpa)

The small, black berries were eaten, collected, and dried for winter by several Native American tribes, including the Mohawk, Huron, Delaware, Cree, Ojibwa, Penobscot, Iroquois, and Chippewa people, who used them like elderberries for relief from colds. Small amounts of berries contain vitamins A, C, and E, iron, folate, and some healthy fiber. They have anti-inflammatory properties. Not the tastiest of berries, they are often sweetened with honey, which can also help with colds. In addition, you can make jelly, syrup, fruit infusions, and even homemade wine with them. Settlers learned from Native Americans and began using chokeberry for coughs, colds, and other conditions such as burns and wounds.

What ailments it helps
Burns
Colds
Coughs
Joint pain
Wound healing

Which part to use
Berries

How to consume it
Syrup: Make syrup from the berries and add for flavor.

Infusions: Use fresh or dried fruit with water. Use one teaspoon of dried fruit in boiling water and strain before drinking.

Tinctures: Make a tincture with berries or infuse the berries in oil for burn treatment or as an anti-inflammatory aid. See PART 7.

Chokecherry
see Wild Black Cherry (89)

24. Cleavers

(Galium aparine)

Round, flat seeds of this herb stick to your clothing if you walk in the countryside. It is also called goosegrass and sticky back. The seeds stick to human clothes and animal fur and are spread and released far away from the mother plant. Native Americans use it for kidney health and gonorrhea. It can flush out toxins, and there are claims it could prevent pregnancy.

What ailments it helps
Bladder irritations
Fluid retention
Liver protection
Stimulates bile production
Urinary tract infections (UTIs)

Which parts to use
All green parts of the plant that grow above the ground (stem and leaves).

How to consume it
Tea: Add a teaspoon of the herb to water, bring to a boil, and leave to steep for 10 minutes. Be sure to strain before drinking. It regularly protects the bladder against irritation and helps with urinary tract infections (UTIs). In addition, studies have shown it stimulates bile production and offers some liver protection. It is also used as a diuretic.

Tincture: You can dry the herb for later use or make a tincture – see PART 7.

25. Coltsfoot

(Tussilago farfara)

This plant is known as horsehoof, bullfoot, British tobacco, and coughwort, as indicated by its use. As a common plant in North and South America, it was most likely introduced by settlers as a medicinal item. For example, the Iroquois used an infusion of its roots to make cough medicine.

What ailments it helps
Bronchitis
Burns
Coughs
Eczema
Fevers
Flu
Insect bites and stings
Skin ulcers
Sore throats
Whooping cough
Wound healing

Which parts to use
Leaves and flowers

How to consume it
Tea: When made into tea, the leaves were used to soothe sore throats, flu, and fever and to treat various skin disorders, from inflammation to burns, skin ulcers, and sores. A poultice of flowers is applied to the skin to treat bites, stings, eczema, etc.

Germany's Commission E has approved using fresh or dried coltsfoot leaf in proprietary products to treat dry cough, hoarseness, and mild throat or mouth inflammations.

NOTES: There are some modern concerns about using this plant's roots, as it contains an alkaloid that may not be beneficial.

26. Comfrey
(Symphytum officinale)

This plant has soft leaves, which are quite hairy. Traditionally, it was called knitbone, as leaves applied externally were used to speed the healing of broken bones; also try an infusion with boneset and nettle. Some studies doubt its internal use, but comfrey is still widely used externally.

What ailments it helps
Broken bone healing
Bruises
Pain relief
Pulled muscles and tendons
Sprains
Wound healing

Which parts to use
Leaves and roots

How to consume it
Ointments: For external use only, use the roots to make an ointment, which provides pain relief. Create your ointment using purchased comfrey oil, if possible.

Poultices: Wrap fresh leaves around an injury for emergency relief. Germany's Commission E positively rated the use of comfrey root (Symphyti radix) for external application to treat bruises, pulled muscles and tendons, and sprains. About ten controlled clinical trials have examined the efficacy and tolerability of topical formulations containing comfrey for pain relief.

"Knitbone" is helpful for application to wounds and injuries that are not healing well.

NOTES: Do not take internally. The plant is known to contain alkaloids that are not desirable for consumption, so use leaves as emergency poultices for sprains and make ointment or oil to use topically.

Cramp Bark
see Black Haw (6)

27. Damiana
(Turnera diffusa)

This small, aromatic shrub is native to the Southern States, including Southern California and Southwestern Texas. It grows wild in Central America, Mexico, South America, and the Caribbean, where an infusion was drunk as an aphrodisiac. Native Americans used this as a relaxing tobacco product combined with wild lettuce. Additionally, it is known to help menstrual cramps, treat nervous conditions, and lift feelings.

What ailments it helps
Abdominal pain
Asthma
Blood pressure
Depression
Joint pains
Libido
Menstrual cramps
Poor appetite
Sleep aid
Stress and anxiety

Which part to use
Fresh or dried leaves

How to consume it
Leaf infusion: Make tea from dried leaves by adding a teaspoon of dried herb to boiling water. Allow it to steep and strain before drinking. Take it three times a day.

WARNING: There are mixed reports on the safety of using damiana while nursing or pregnant, so do not use without consulting your herbalist or doctor.

28. Dandelion

see PART 4

29. Devil's Claw

(Harpagophytum procumbens)

The "claw" name comes from its long protrusions with "hooks" that can cause injury to humans and animals. These secondary roots, known as tubers, grow out of the primary roots used in herbal medicine. The plant was widely used by the Apache, Cahuilla, Hopi, Yaqui, Pima, and Shoshone people. For example, the stems are used to make baskets by many tribes. However, its primary medical use was to ease pain due to inflammation, both externally and inside the body. Modern medicine backs this up, and the herb is often used to ease arthritic or rheumatic pain and muscle aches. Devil's claw is used in Germany as a topical ointment, and tea from it can be good for headaches.

Recent studies recommend not taking devil's claw for an extended period. 8-12 week pain relief programs for patients with osteoarthritis have been tried in the US and were found to bring great relief. However, it is not advisable to continue the use of devil's claw for longer than this.

What ailments it helps
Boils and sores
Gout
Headaches
Inflammation
Muscle pain
Osteoarthritis
Rheumatism

Which parts to use
Tuberous roots and stems

How to consume it
Tuberous roots can be dried and grated, infused into oil or tinctures, or added to creams.

Tincture: For aches and pains, use a tincture or liquid extract in water to ease muscle pain or spread ointment on the skin topically. See PART 7.

Infusion: For headaches, make an herb infusion or swallow drops of the tincture or liquid extract with water. Make an infusion by drying the root and grating it into smaller pieces. Then add a teaspoon to a cup of water, bring to a boil, steep for 5 minutes, then strain and drink. Use a commercially bought liquid extract or tincture if this is more convenient. See PART 7 for how to make ointments, tinctures, and infusions.

WARNING: Avoid if pregnant. In addition, the plant may interact with some medicines (blood thinners, anticoagulants, etc.), so discuss with your herbalist or medical professional before taking it.

---

30. Dogwood
(Cornus florida)

The colorful twigs of dogwood brighten up any garden in winter, but Native Americans used the inner bark and the twigs for various medicinal uses. For example, they used it widely to reduce fevers. In the South during the Civil War, it was used for malarial fever and chronic diarrhea. Dogwood was also used to treat pneumonia and colds. The Cherokee commonly used it for headaches, and the Iroquois used dogwood tonic for gonorrhea. The Menominee used the bark in enemas.

What ailments it helps
Colds
Diarrhea
Fevers
Gonorrhea
Headaches
Improve appetite
Malaria
Measles
Pneumonia
Wound healing

Which parts to use
The bark and twigs

How to consume it
Decoction: Use the twigs to make a decoction – see PART 7.

Poultices: Used externally, the Cherokee made poultices for wounds and other skin disorders using the bark – see PART 7.

Ceremonial use: The Arikara mixed the dried inner bark with uva ursi to make sacred tobacco for ceremonies.

31. Echinacea
(Echinacea angustifolia)

Echinacea, also known as the purple coneflower for the unique shape of its flower, was widely used by many Native American tribes. The Kiowa chewed the roots to ease coughs and sore throats, which is still a practice today. Studies have been conducted using this plant as a cold remedy, and people taking this tincture experienced significantly fewer and milder symptoms.

The Ute observed wild elks digging up the root when they were wounded. This symbolism gave power to its healing properties, and coneflower roots were used in the Great Plains to treat pain and wounds and ease swelling. Tribe members chewed echinacea during ceremonies in sweat lodges. The Navajo revere the use of coneflower as a sacred Life Medicine, and the Cheyenne made leaf infusions for sore throats and also for mouth sores. The Choctaw chewed roots and also made a tincture for coughs.

What ailments it helps
Colds
Coughs
Inflammation
Mouth sores
Pain relief
Shingles
Sore throats
Upper respiratory infections
Wound healing

Which parts to use
Roots and leaves

How to consume it
Dig a portion of root and dry it, then grate or powder it and store it out of direct sunlight. Chew it when symptoms present.

Tincture: Make a tincture from an extract of the root – see how to make this in PART 7. Add drops of the tincture to water and drink daily.

Infusions: Use the leaves to make an infusion and drink daily for sore throats and mouth sores – see PART 7.

NOTES: Only take echinacea for up to 10 days for colds, etc., as its efficacy after this time has been shown to drop. Take after food.

32. Elderflower
see PART 4

33. Evening Primrose
(Oenothera biennis)

Evening primrose is a tall-stemmed plant native to the Eastern and Northern US and used by Native Americans for centuries. It was used for respiratory ailments, as a wound cleaner for skin, and as a dietary supplement. In addition, they spread the pungent smell of the plant on shoes to disguise the scent of humans when they were hunting. Finally, this plant provided food and medicine for the Cherokee, Iroquois, Ojibwa, and Potawatomi people. Tender, first-year leaves are wonderful when added to salads, and the taste is even more improved by cooking in other dishes.

The origins of evening primrose are not very distinct; the plant was unknown in Europe until about the 18th century, when settlers took seeds from America. Modern studies show that menstrual discomfort and menopausal symptoms are aided by using this herb in the daily diet or added as a supplement.

What ailments it helps

Fevers
Menopausal symptoms
Menstrual discomfort
Respiratory ailments
Skin problems
Wound healing

Which parts to use

Leaves, flowers, stems, seeds, and roots

How to consume it

Use as a dietary supplement (processed from various parts of the plant) to treat the ailments mentioned. Taken as an infusion or as oil, the supplements provide gamma-linoleic and essential oils, which the body must ingest daily for a healthy metabolism. An infusion of leaves provides flavonoids and supplements the diets of Native Americans.

Food: Use the young leaves (tastier in the first year of growth) in the spring before the tree flowers, and add them to salads. The taste is even more improved when cooked, so add them to soups, etc. Seeds can be added to bread mixes, cereals, salads, and baking.

Roots: Dig up a root and use it like potatoes, boiled or baked. Peel them before eating.

NOTES: This plant spreads rapidly due to the many seeds produced and can become out of control, so beware!

34. (American) Feverfew
(Parthenium integrifolium)

Two varieties of this herb are discussed here. This one, American Feverfew, is also known as wild quinine. The second Feverfew (no. 35) is a different plant of European origin, which grows in the US and is known to help migraine sufferers. Both plants were used for headache relief and to bring down fevers.

What ailments it helps

Burns
Fevers
Fluid retention
Headaches (migraines)

Which part to use

Leaves

How to consume it

Fresh leaves can be made into an infusion, a poultice, or eaten in salads. Fresh leaves can be dried to have a supply in winter. Pick stems when the plant is growing actively in summer, and dry. In warmer climates, the plant will remain in winter. However, it is not generally tolerant of frost.

Poultice: Make a poultice and apply with leaves directly to the burn to soothe it – see PART 7.

Diuretic for fluid retention: Make an infusion with leaves.

35. Feverfew
(Tanacetum parthenium)

In the mid-19th century, feverfew was introduced in the United States. The plant grows along roadsides, fields, waste areas, and the borders of woods from eastern Canada to Maryland and westward to Missouri.

What ailments it helps

Fevers
Headaches (migraines)

Which part to use

Leaves

How to consume it

Fresh leaves are eaten, but in some cases, they can cause mouth allergies, so it is probably best to make an infusion with leaves and drink it if you feel the onset of a migraine. This herb is frost tolerant, although it will die in deep snow over extended periods. There can occasionally be side effects, so to be extra-safe Jacob suggests purchasing dried leaves or using a recognized herbalist to create your preparation.

NOTES: Canada recently approved encapsulated feverfew leaves for migraine as an over-the counter pharmaceutical.

WARNING: Avoid if pregnant.

36. Feverwort
(Triosteum perfoliatum)

This plant is known as fever root, wild coffee, and tinker's weed. It grows natively in eastern parts of the US. The Cherokee used this herb to bring down a fever, among other medicinal uses. The dried seeds or berries were ground and used in other tribes as a hot drink, a coffee substitute, although it does not resemble the real thing. The plant prefers rich soils and a shady position.

What ailments it helps

Backache
Diarrhea
Fevers
Flu symptoms
Joint pain
Nausea
Pleurisy
Skin irritations

Which parts to use

Leaves, roots, and seeds

How to consume it

Decoction of leaves for a fever.

An infusion of the root for flu symptoms or upset stomach – can also be used to soak sore feet or in a bath. Use as a poultice of the root for skin irritations. Dried and roasted seeds as a hot drink substitute (though it may not be to everyone's taste!). See PART 7 for recipes.

37. Flaxseed
see PART 4

38. Garlic *(Allium sativum)* and Wild Garlic *(Allium tricoccum)*

Garlic

Wild Garlic

Garlic grows as a bulb and has a distinctive taste in cooking worldwide. Wild garlic bulbs from the same family are native to Canada, South Carolina, Missouri, and Minnesota. Native Americans drank garlic tea for its medicinal benefits. Modern research shows that garlic helps lower cholesterol, and bulbs have been used to treat asthma, emphysema, rheumatism, and diarrhea. In addition, garlic capsules are used for treating high blood pressure. Eating garlic regularly is claimed to help prevent colds. The Blackfeet of Western Montana use wild garlic, among other herbs, to help ease the symptoms of Parkinson's Disease.

What ailments it helps
Arthritis
Asthma
Colds
Diarrhea
Emphysema
High blood pressure
High cholesterol
Intestinal worms
Parkinson's Disease
Rheumatism
Ringworm
Stimulates breast milk flow
Stomach ulcers

Which part to use
Bulbs

How to consume it
External use: Grind raw bulbs into a pulp and apply directly onto sore joints. Cover with gauze or a bandage.

Food: When used in cooking, it lowers cholesterol, lowers high blood pressure, eases various breathing disorders, and helps prevent/ease common colds.

Garlic tea: Use ground or whole bulbs in hot infusions. If you dislike the taste, buy and use garlic capsules. But as always, Jacob pleads that you buy organic.

39. Gentiana

(Gentiana andrewsii)

This pretty blue flowering plant usually settles in shady woodland. It is native to Northeastern North America, from the Dakotas to the East Coast and Eastern Canada. Gentiana is also known as bitter root and bitter wort, revealing the part of the plant used medicinally. Native Americans used this extremely bitter herb to lower fevers. The Iroquois people used an infusion of dried roots to soothe headaches, and the Catawba heated the roots in water and applied the mixture to the skin. In addition, Gentiana has anti-fungal, anti-inflammatory, and anti-hepatic properties and is ideally used for wound care. Finally, it is an antidote for snakebites. Despite the bitter taste, it can stimulate appetite and treat stomach problems for those recovering from long illnesses. Currently, gentiana is an ingredient in many cleansing products and cosmetics and is regarded as one of the best plants to use in cases of weakness and lack of appetite.

What ailments it helps

Digestive ailments
Fevers
Headaches
Intestinal worms
Joint pain
Malaria
Muscle and back aches
Snakebites
Stimulate appetite
Wound healing

Which part to use

Roots

How to consume it

Infusions: Fresh or dried roots were used to make tea, treat wounds externally, or drink to stimulate appetite.

NOTES: Use caution if you have ulcers, as this plant may cause nausea, vomiting, or headaches.

Ginger

see Wild Ginger (91)

40. (American) Ginseng

(Panax quinquefolius)

Ginseng Roots

American ginseng is an endangered species in some parts of the US, although it still grows wild in some wooded areas in Eastern regions and Southeastern Canada, so grow it at home from seeds or seek a reputable permitted supplier. The Cherokee used this plant to make root teas to stimulate appetite, help heal from long illnesses, and for pain relief from headaches and earaches. Other Native American tribes used the plant as a tonic for female infertility, digestive problems, and treating fevers. It was also used as a poultice for skin conditions. American ginseng was picked, dried, and stored by the Cherokee, so it was available when needed.

What ailments it helps
Appetite stimulant
Boils and sores
Digestive problems
Earaches
Fevers
Headaches
Memory function
Muscle cramps
Pain relief

Which part to use
Roots

How to consume it
Tea: Slice the root into small parts and simmer in warm water (not boiling) for about 45 mins or longer. Ensure to strain before drinking. Useful for the ailments listed, and it's an appetite stimulant for the elderly or those recuperating from illness.

Poultice: Apply a poultice on the boils and use direct contact with any painful areas of the skin.

NOTES: Difficult to acquire in the wild, so purchasing supplements may be easier in some cases.

WARNING: Avoid taking orally while pregnant.

41. Goldenrod
(Solidago spp.)

This tall yellow flower was widely used as a medicine among Native Americans to cure respiratory ailments, heal wounds, and help recover from colds and sore throats. The Chippewa named it "sun medicine" and used it to provide relief from boils, ulcers, and also fevers. The Cherokee also infused the plant to reduce fever. The Algonquin used it for heart disease, and its Latin name translates as "to make whole." All parts of the goldenrod plant are functional.

What ailments it helps
Bladder problems
Boils
Colds
Fevers
Gout
Nasal congestion
Sore throats
Sores / ulcers
Wound healing

Which parts to use
Leaves, flowers, stems, and roots

How to consume it
Plant infusion: Drink the infused tea to reduce a fever, soothe sore throats, and for nasal congestion. You can also make a steam bath for respiratory congestion by adding the liquid to a

basin, placing a towel over a basin, and inhaling the steam. Traditionally, goldenrod was boiled and used in sweat lodge ceremonies.

Root infusion: Use fresh or dried roots.

Poultice: Use fresh leaves for boils, applying them directly to the affected area – see PART 7.

42. Goldenseal
(Hydrastis canadensis)

Plant

Dried Root

This woodland plant produces tiny white flowers in spring, and the small, red berries look similar to raspberries; however, this fruit is not edible. Goldenseal has many local names, including Indian dye, yellow root, eye root, yellow puccoon, wild curcuma, and wild turmeric, and when you see the roots, you can guess why. They are bright yellow, the same color as turmeric spice. The Native American need for this plant was mainly concerned with collecting the rhizome roots for their medicinal use. For example, the roots of goldenseal contain resin, oil, hydrastine, berberine, and canadine. Also, you can make yellow dye by boiling the roots. The Cherokee used the plant as a cancer cure, an antidote for snakebite, and an antiseptic for wounds. The Iroquois treated whooping cough with goldenseal and used a root preparation mixed with grease as an insect repellent. In addition, the roots are used as an eyewash for infections and soothing sore throats.

What ailments it helps
Cancer
Eye infections
Intestinal worms
Snakebites
Sore throats
Stomach ulcers
Tooth infection
Whooping cough
Wound healing

Which part to use
Roots

How to consume it
Root tea infusion as an eyewash: Infuse grated root in boiling water. Strain the liquid, cool it, and use it on the eyes.

Root tea infusion for sore throats: Steep for 10 minutes, then strain and gargle with the mixture to ease a scratchy throat.

Root tea infusion for toothache: Drink 3 cups (0.71 l) per day maximum. It is said to have anti-inflammatory properties like turmeric.

Insect repellent: Roots grated into grease and applied topically repels insects. Roots, dried and made into powder, were used for wound treatment.

NOTES: Some herbalists maintain that there are toxic substances in goldenseal, so do not give it to young children. Take in small quantities, and not for a prolonged period of time.

WARNING: Avoid if pregnant.

43. Gravel Root / Joe Pye Weed
(Eupatorium purpureum)

Gravel root refers to the kidney or bladder stones the plant is supposed to remove. Joe Pye is a historical Native American healer who resided in Massachusetts. Others reference the name of this plant to the Native American word for typhus: jopi or jopai.

The Cherokee and Iroquois used the plant as a diuretic. The Cherokee used only the roots and flowers. Gravel Root is known to increase sweating and thereby reduce fevers, too. Tea made from the roots and the tops of the green plant was used as remedies for gout, diarrhea, and impotence. If you grow Joe Pye weed in your flower garden, you will invite swarms of pollinators, as bees adore the flowers.

What ailments it helps
Diarrhea
Fevers
Fluid retention
Gout

Which parts to use
Roots, flowers, tops, and stems

How to consume it
Infusion: Make an infusion with the leaves and strain before drinking.

Use dried, grated, or fresh roots. Allow brewing for 10 minutes and strain before drinking.

Burn some stems with leaves as a mosquito repellent. You can also make yellow dye from this plant.

44. Hawthorn
(Crataegus spp.)

The Iroquois used the twigs and branches (without leaves) in infusions for stomach problems and as a preventative method to avoid cancer, believed to occur by evil magic or witchcraft. Many Native Americans ate the fruit because they contain anti-inflammatory and antioxidant properties. Berries are still eaten today in many places worldwide. Bark, sapwood, and the roots were utilized in decoctions by the Okanagan for stomach issues, and this shrub was a tonic to build good health, particularly in recovery after an illness. Recent studies have shown that hawthorn tea may benefit those with high blood pressure. The Okanagan and the Thompson population ate the berries.

What ailments it helps
Cold sores
Heart problems
High blood pressure
Indigestion
Joint pain
Stomach problems

A general good health tonic to ease anxiety and for any condition that makes one restless.

Which parts to use
Twigs, branches, bark, sapwood, roots, and berries

How to consume it
Infusion: Make an infusion from fresh spring shoots, then gargle with it to aid cold sores or as a general tonic; strain before drinking.

Children's health: Make an oral infusion of new shoots for diarrhea. This same infusion helps rinse out small mouths with sores.

Decoction: Make a decoction from the bark or roots for stomach issues – see PART 7.

Food: Pick ripe berries to eat or make jelly or jam.

NOTES: If suffering from heart problems, consult with an herbalist and make them aware of any physician-prescribed medications before taking hawthorn.

Always check with your medical practitioner before giving herbal remedies to children.

45. Hemlock: Western Hemlock *(Tsuga heterophylla)* and Eastern Hemlock *(Tsuga canadensis)*

Western Hemlock

Eastern Hemlock

Two native hemlock trees grow in the Eastern and Western US. Tsuga heterophylla can be found in forests of the Pacific Northwest, whereas Tsuga canadensis is located in the Eastern US and Canada.

Both trees are featured in the legends of Native Americans. The stories told by the Micmac and Seneca peoples can be read today. They believe it's essential to understand better the interconnection with the natural world we experience and the magical qualities the trees provide. These enormous trees provided shelter, wood, medical uses, and a connection to nature and were valued by Native Americans.

For example, tannin from the bark was used in tanning leather and wool products. Today, the wood of the hemlock is valuable in the lumber industry.

Early records say that Native Americans used eastern hemlock both as sunscreen and to soothe sunburned skin.

What ailments it helps
Colds
Coughs
Diarrhea
Fevers
Flu
Rheumatism
Scurvy
Sunscreen / burn
Wound healing

Which parts to use
Leaves (the green needles), twigs, and bark

How to consume it
Infusion: Use twigs steeped in boiling water to make tea. The tea's vapors are inhaled to relieve coughs, colds, and rheumatism.

Make bark tea to treat diarrhea, as well as colds and fevers. In the past, tea was used to treat scurvy.

Poultices: Tannins in the twigs have astringent qualities. Bark pieces can be placed on a wounded area and covered with gauze or a bandage to stop bleeding and speed healing.

NOTES: There is a European Hemlock plant with the same name. However, European Hemlock is a poisonous shrub, not a huge tree.

46. Honeysuckle
(Lonicera ciliosa, hispidula, sempervirens)

Ciliosa

Three types of honeysuckle grow wild in the US. The first is an orange-flowered variety that grows in the Western States. The second is a pink flower plant that also grows in the West. Then there's the red honeysuckle, which extends along the Eastern and Southern US. All three are extremely useful in Native American medicine.

Sometimes you may notice a Japanese variety, but they are considered invasive and not native to the area. No matter which variety, the flowers are edible, but the berries can be poisonous. The stems and vines of the plants are not usually edible.

What ailments it helps
Asthma
Coughs
Digestive disorders
Fevers
Sore throats

Which part to use
Flowers

How to consume it
Food: Cut the flowers carefully because the nectar or "honey" will leak out if you cut the end of the flower. Eat the delicious "honey" straight from the flowers when they're in bloom.

Jelly: Make honeysuckle jelly from the flowers.

Add sugar and water with flowers, boil until the mixture sets, and seal in containers for use.

Syrup: Make a syrup to soothe sore throats – see PART 7.

Infusion: Make an infusion of fresh flowers to soothe sore throats and ease digestive disorders. You can also dry the flowers for winter.

NOTES: Only some varieties of shrubs have edible berries, so if in doubt, please avoid.

47. Hops
(Humulus lupulus)

This climbing plant with twining stems has branches that twist around each other as they grow, up to 30 ft (9.14 m) high. It is well-known for its flavor, providing beer's unique taste. In addition, its edible young shoots and leaves serve as food during famines.

The Native Americans used hops as a sedative to help insomnia and relieve toothache. In addition, it is known to contain antibacterial compounds and was also used as a poultice on boils and to reduce swelling.

Flowers appear in the spring in greenish clusters, both male and female, but on different plants. Once pollination occurs, the female ones transform into cones for harvesting. They appear to have overlapping parts, which turn brown in the fall and resemble pine cones. These grow wild in hedges, or you can grow your own to ensure no sprays or pesticides contaminate them. The young green cones are edible, along with the young heart-shaped leaves.

What ailments it helps
Antibacterial
Anxiety
Boils
Insomnia
Sedative
Swelling
Toothache

Which parts to use
Female cones and leaves

How to consume it
Poultice: A poultice of female cones can reduce swellings using wrappings of the herb.

A poultice or wrapping of female cones will draw out the contents of a boil. Discard the herb after use and replace it with new fresh growth twice a day until the area looks clean.

Powder: You can also dry the brown cones each fall when they are in season. Grate the dry cones into powder and store them in a closed container. See how to make a healing ointment from hops in PART 7.

Infusion: Use dried hops to make an infusion for insomnia or as a mild sedative, or sip to ease toothache.

48. Horsemint
(Monarda punctata)

Also known as spotted bee balm horsemint for the attractive flowers loved by bees, it comes in various colors. Many Native Americans used the leaves and flowering stems in teas, tonics, and ointments for wound healing. Often used for rheumatism and arthritis, Native Americans used a poultice of the plant to encourage healing. Its active ingredient, thymol, can be saved in essential oil – see PART 7. Apply the antiseptic oil directly to the wounds.

What ailments it helps
Arthritis
Congestion
Fevers
Flatulence
Fluid retention
Indigestion
Nausea
Respiratory problems
Rheumatism
Wound healing

Which parts to use
Leaves and flowering stems

How to consume it
Leaves and flowering stems are used in teas, tonics, and salves for various medical issues. For example, it helps pain from rheumatism and joint pain in arthritis by increasing blood to the area and flushing out toxins due to its diuretic properties.

Infusion: Make an infusion with fresh or dried leaves to treat digestive disorders, congestion and respiratory issues, and reduce fevers.

Ointments: Make essential oil from leaves or flowers for healing ointments to use topically on wounds.

WARNING: Avoid if pregnant.

49. Horsetail
(Equisetum arvense)

Also known as shavegrass, Native Americans and early settlers made tea as a diuretic and cough medicine for horses. It was also used for scouring and polishing objects and as a dye for clothing, lodges, and porcupine quills. Additionally, the young shoots were eaten either cooked or raw.

What ailments it helps
Burns
Fluid retention
Gout
Jaundice
Kidney and bladder stones
Osteoarthritis
Prostate conditions
Reduces bleeding

Rheumatism
Urinary tract infections (UTIs)
Wound healing

Which parts to use
Leaves and stems

How to consume it
Infusion: Add 1-2 teaspoonfuls of the leaves to boiling water and steep for 5-10 minutes. Then strain before serving. Drink one or two cups daily.

First aid: Apply the green leaves and stem to a wound for emergency first aid.

To reduce blood flow: To reduce the strength of heavy period blood flow, to stop nosebleeds, or to soothe hemorrhage in lungs and stomach, drink an infusion.

NOTES: Do not exceed the dosage. Do not use if cardiac or renal dysfunction is present.

50. Juniper
(Juniperus communis)

Juniper is a common evergreen shrub on hillsides and mountains in North America, Europe, and Asia. There are over 40 varieties of juniper. The tree forms blue-colored berries in the fall, consumed by Native Americans for many conditions. Find the small, round, blue-colored berries that grow in the fall and early winter. The essential oil made from ripe, dry berries aids digestion and helps to prevent heartburn, cramp, and indigestion.

Some of their berries are considered safe for eating in small quantities cooked in a stew or with fatty meat to aid digestion. However, you should carefully identify the shrub, as some juniper berries are unsuitable for consumption.

Twigs and branches can be burned for their scent and used in ceremonies and purification of spaces.

The Pueblo people of the Southwestern States used juniper twigs. They placed the twigs over a fire and toasted them, then used them as binding over bruises or sprains to reduce swelling and pain. The Santa Clara Pueblo is reported to have used juniper gum as a natural filling for rotten teeth. The Cree have used it as a diuretic. In addition, the Comanche and the Salish used the plant as a disinfectant. Many tribes widely used it as an anti-rheumatic and cold remedy, including the Chippewa, Dakota, Delaware, and Iroquois. The oil of the juniper is an anti-inflammatory applied to arthritic joints. The Hopi collected the fresh gum from the tree and used it to draw out infection and sterilize a wound or cut. Many Southwestern tribes used this gum for similar purposes.

Juniper is included in the British Pharmacopeia for use as a urinary tract antiseptic to relieve benign urinary infections.

Juniper was used in ceremonies and the baptism of newborn infants to purify both child and mother. Steam room use of juniper is still common, and its fresh smell, mainly when burning, provides a perfect wood for smudging ceremonies. The Navajo used juniper twigs to smooth out their footprints and paths after burials so the devil could not follow them from their burial site.

What ailments it helps

Arthritis
Colds
Fluid retention
Heartburn
Indigestion
Inflammation
Pain
Prostate issues
Rheumatism
Stomach cramps
Urinary tract infections (UTIs)
Wound healing

Which parts to use

Berries, twigs, branches, and gum

How to consume it

Food: In cooking, consume berries in small quantities. However, remember to carefully identify the berries you choose to eat because there are some poisonous varieties; Juniperus sabina is considered toxic.

Some herbalists advise consuming no more than one berry a day, but generally, either use a commercial tincture or team up with an expert when picking.

Tincture: For the ailments listed, use 12 drops of berry tincture in a mug of water up to three times per day.

Healing oil: Use the oil and spread it on wounds and sore areas for rheumatic pain relief. See PART 7 for advice on how to make healing oils.

WARNING: Avoid if pregnant – has been known to cause miscarriages.

51. (Desert) Lavender

(Condea emoryi)

This lavender is not the European lavender we all know so well, which is not native to the Americas, having been brought over by settlers in the 1800s. Instead, this herb is desert lavender, also known as lavender bushmint, with purple-colored flowers and grayish foliage. It is a large, herbaceous shrub native to Southern California, Arizona, and New Mexico. It was revered by the Native American people who lived there not only because of its medicinal value but also for its ceremonial uses. For example, the Cahuilla people used the purple flowers to create an infusion to heal the body. Likewise, the Seni use it today for smudging to clear the body of disease and protect it from evil forces.

What ailments it helps

Antioxidant for the liver, e.g., due to chemical sensitivities or a hangover
Anxiety
Colds
Coughs
Flu
Gastric ulcers
Heartburn
Hemorrhages
Insomnia
Menorrhagia (very heavy or overly long menstrual bleeding)
Peptic ulcers
Skin irritations

Which parts to use

Leaves and flowers. Collect whenever in flower, which can be any time of year, though they are more abundant in spring. You can either remove the leaves and flowers or, if young and flexible, collect the stems with leaves and flowers still attached. Fresh or dried, they can be stored loosely in paper bags in a cool place safe from direct sunlight. Stems with leaves (no flowers) for smudging.

How to consume it

Tea: Use as a hot or cold infusion (4-8 oz per day), preferably made with the fresh plant.

Tincture: The fresh or dried plant can be made with a higher ratio of flowers to leaves. Consume up to 30 drops daily in water – see PART 7 for the tincture recipe.

Ointment / salve: Use externally for skin conditions – see PART 7.

For smudging: Use fresh, leafy stems without flowers, bundle them together with string or yarn, and let dry out before use.

52. Lemon Balm
(Melissa officinalis)

This herb prefers to grow in the shade and has a slightly minty scent. It can be invasive if grown in a garden, so it is best grown in a pot. The Cherokee called it "wa du li si" or bee, and its soothing properties lend themselves well to both salves and infusions. If possible, harvest just before flowering for the herb to be at its most potent.

What ailments it helps

Anxiety
Cold sores
Headaches
Indigestion (including bloating and gas)
Insect bites
Insomnia
Menstrual cramps
Reducing stress
Sweating (to reduce)

Which part to use

Leaves

How to consume it

Make a tea from the leaves, fresh or dried. Add honey to taste.

As an infusion, lemon balm tea helps to relax the body and mind before sleeping. It can reduce sweating, ease indigestion, and help alleviate pain.

They are sometimes used in combination with other healing herbs (e.g., chamomile, valerian, hops) in lotions and infusions.

Make a salve or ointment on cold sores, insect bites, and burns – see PART 7.

53. Mesquite
(Prosopis glandulosa)

This tree is native to semi-arid climates in North America and grows in similar environments in Argentina, India, and South Africa. It provided Native Americans with a unique flour, ground from the ripe, yellow pods mixed with water to make bread, and was also added to cooking. Mesquite beans are harvested when they turn hard and golden. Then, the pods and seeds are ground into a meal. This process is still commonly practiced today in parts of Arizona. The tree tolerates low rainfall well and is a nitrogen fixer, which means it improves the fertility of the soil where it grows. The Pima reputedly used the dark sap as hair dye, allowing it to soak in overnight. They also used needles from the tree's thorns to sew clothes.

The gum of the tree mended pottery when used as an adhesive. Native American medical use of mesquite included using the flowers in hot tea to soothe sore throats, eating its leaves, and the twigs were cooked to release the resin to soothe stings, wounds, and insect bites. Bees adored the flowers, and their honey had the distinct taste of the tree. In addition, the wood was used for arrows and hunting equipment.

What ailments it helps
Sore throats
Stings and bites
Wound healing

Which parts to use
Flowers, pods, gum, and sap

How to consume it
Make a refreshing tea from the fresh or dried flowers to soothe sore throats. Ensure to strain before drinking.

Collect the gum for use on wounds, stings, and bites.

Food: Pods and seeds can be ground into meal, and beans can be eaten. It is gluten-free, so it is suitable for celiacs.

54. Milkweed
(Asclepias spp.)

This plant was used widely in making fiber and textiles, which were made into clothing by many Native Americans. In addition, the plant is grown commercially as padding for coats to improve insulation. Milkweed is poisonous if consumed, but the plant has been used in Native American healing for removing warts. It also has wound healing benefits and can be made into ointments.

What ailments it helps
Ringworm treatment
Wart removal
Wound healing

Which part to use
The toxic sap from the stem once it is picked.

How to consume it
Make an ointment with the sap you can collect by cutting the plant. Apply externally to heal wounds and treat ringworm.

Spread the "raw" sap on the wart's surface over several applications. It may discolor at first, and you can remove this part, discard it, and then re-apply until the wart has disappeared.

WARNING: It is dangerous if consumed internally. Do not eat this plant, as it is poisonous.

55. Mint
see PART 4

56. Mullein
(Verbascum thapsus)

Native Americans made root decoctions with mullein to reduce swelling in painful arthritic joints. Fresh or dried mullein flowers improve asthma, coughs, and respiratory conditions; they can be used fresh or dried. Tea made from mullein was used in cough mixtures as it has expectorant and soothing properties and can fight infection.

What ailments it helps
Antibacterial
Anti-inflammatory
Antiviral
Asthma
Bronchitis
Colds
Congestion
Coughs
Earache
Flu
Painful muscles
Respiratory problems
Sore throats
Tinnitus
Wound healing

Which parts to use
Flowers (fresh or dried), huge velvety soft, fresh leaves, and roots

How to consume it
Mullein tea: Use flowers (fresh or dried) to make infusions. Strain the tea before drinking. Another use for this tea is as a cleanser for wounds, and it is placed directly in the ear to soothe earache. Adding honey makes a great sore throat cure.

Use fresh leaves as shoe insoles to keep your feet wrapped in antibacterial, natural comfort.

For wounds, apply leaves for their antiviral and antibacterial benefits and pain-relieving and anti-inflammatory properties.

The roots are used to make a decoction by adding 4 tablespoons (56.7 g) of finely chopped root and simmering in a quart (.95 l) of water for around a half hour. After it sits, strain it and consume 4-8 oz (118-236 ml) three times daily.

57. Nettle
(Urtica dioica)

Native Americans have used nettles for food and medicine. It is widely used around the world due to its ability to stop bleeding. In addition, it is used as a tonic in springtime to provide valuable minerals to purify the blood and the liver. The leaves are gently rubbed before applying to wounds to stop excessive bleeding and dried and powdered for wound care. The nettle plant has other uses, too. The Omaha, the Cupeño from Southern California, and the Menominee from Wisconsin and Michigan all used this plant for clothes such as cloaks, ponchos, and undershirts. Close to fishing areas, they made the plant into fishing nets. Native Americans associate the nettle with the coyote and, therefore, as the trickster of their stories. The same is reported in Mexico and the Mayan world. A Cree story describes how this plant used to have a different color, but due to being ignored by humanity, it chose to change to green to appear like other foliage. The stinging hairs reminded humanity each time skin was stung that this plant is not one to be ignored. Indeed, there are traditions, not only in America, of using the sting in urtication, a process where a person uses stems with stinging leaves to beat the naked back to stimulate healing. Medical opinion is not certain of the benefits, but the tradition has a 2,000-year-old history.

Commission E in Germany has approved nettle use for therapy for rheumatism, and many tribes in Nevada are known to have burned nettle leaves in sweat lodges. The ceremonial use is similar to the use of tobacco, sage, and other sacred herbs, with the inhalation of burning nettles assisting in healing pneumonia and flu infections.

Another use for nettle was among Native American women, who used it to ease labor pain and reduce excessive bleeding during childbirth, as well as stimulate the flow of breast milk. Nettle is known to stop bleeding and was also used for wound binding. In an infusion, nettle, boneset, and comfrey offer an aid to healing broken bones.

What ailments it helps
Broken bones
Flu
Labor pains
Painful joints
Pneumonia
Prostate issues
Rheumatism
Spring tonic for blood and liver health
Stimulates breast milk flow
Stops bleeding
Wound healing

Which parts to use

Leaves: Pick when young and fresh in late winter and early spring. Make sure you wear gloves to avoid stings.

Stems: You can dry stems, remove the outer layer, and use this to make ropes and fabric.

Roots: Bright orange roots can be carefully dug up and then preserved in tinctures, dried for infusions, and used in rope making. Be mindful when removing roots; remember not to remove the whole root.

How to consume it

Wound healing: Leaves can be applied directly to wounds, but to avoid stinging, wear gloves and rub the leaves gently to remove hairs. Leaves can be dried, powdered, and used on wounds to stop bleeding. Also, a nettle root tincture can be applied to wounds – see PART 7 for directions.

Nettle tea: Carefully pick stems and dry the leaves, then add a teaspoon of dried leaves to boiling water. Strain the leaves before drinking. Tea is also made from dried nettle roots.

Soup: Young spring leaves can be made into nettle soup, providing a source of iron and potassium. Boil water and drop leaves in, then discard this water after the leaves have stewed for 5 minutes, thereby removing the sting. After this, continue to simmer the leaves for 10 minutes until the leaves look like cooked spinach. Use a food processor to mix the liquid into a soup and add a dash of cream, black pepper, and salt to taste.

Nettle tonic: This provides the perfect way to uplift the spirits and purify the blood. Make it from fresh new spring leaf growth. Pick enough to fill two dessert spoons and warm this gently in boiling water. Discard the first water to remove the sting, add fresh water, and heat gently. Do not boil too long as this removes the vitamins.

58. Oak
(Quercus rubra)

The acorn from this tree was a staple food of many tribes. For example, acorn porridge was often prescribed for people recovering from tuberculosis without vaccination or protection. For the Native American medical chest, the tree's bark was boiled into a decoction to treat diarrhea and used to gargle and soothe a sore throat.

What ailments it helps

Appetite stimulant after illness
Diarrhea
Joint swelling
Kidney and bladder problems
Skin irritations
Sore throats
Sprains

Which parts to use

Inner tree bark, acorns, and leaves

How to consume it

Use the inner bark to make a decoction – see PART 7. For sore throats, add drops of this to water to gargle or to bathe skin conditions.

Use the inner bark to make an infusion, and use as a drink for digestive issues and to bathe skin irritations.

Poultices: Make with leaves and use to ease swelling and sprains.

Food: Acorns and acorn porridge for convalescence after illness.

Bark, acorn, and leaves can be dried and ground into powder, and used on skin irritations.

59. Oats
(Avena sativa) and
Wild Oats
(Chasmanthium latifolium)

Avena Sativa

Chasmanthium Latifolium

Often called oat straw, this grassy plant is called groats, herb oats, oat grass, and wild oats. It is an ancient food source for humans and animals. Modern scientific research shows how beneficial oats are for many medical conditions, including their ability to lower cholesterol. It is an excellent food to stabilize blood sugar, which explains why it is recommended for people with diabetes. It seems to increase vigor and stamina, and a tincture will help to ease nervousness, exhaustion, and insomnia. In addition, it is effective in treating multiple sclerosis, ADHD, tumors, and diabetes. Regular consumption has been linked to lessening the risk of colon cancer.

What ailments it helps
ADHD
Cancer
Diabetes
Exhaustion
Insomnia
Lowers cholesterol
Multiple Sclerosis
Nervousness
Stabilizes blood sugar

Which part to use
The seed heads are processed and flattened to make porridge oats.

How to consume it
Food: Eat it as porridge. Soak the seeds in water and cook them over low heat. Make a tincture – see PART 7.

60. Oregon Grape
(Mahonia aquifolium)

Various Oregon grape species are medicinally important. Native American tribes of the Pacific Northwest have used preparations from Oregon grape roots to treat stomach problems, hemorrhages, arthritis, and tuberculosis. Boiling the roots and inner bark of Oregon grape produces a yellow dye used on wool. The Nlaka'pamux people of British Columbia applied it to their basketry.

What ailments it helps
Arthritis
Gastrointestinal problems
Hemorrhages
Intestinal worms
Tuberculosis

Which part to use
Golden yellow roots

How to consume it
Use roots to create an infusion and drink it as tea for its medicinal properties. Limit to 3 cups (0.71l) per day.

Make into a tincture and add to water. Limit to 3 cups (0.71 l) per day.

61. Osha
(Ligusticum porteri)

Osha in Flower

Dried Osha Root

Osha is often called bear root because Native American people observed bears eating it immediately after waking from hibernation. In post-hibernation, bears are hungry, possibly malnourished, and need energy, so as a readily available natural food source, this is ideal for bears (and humans). Other names for this herb are chuchupate, Indian parsley, Porter's lovage, and Colorado cough root, which give an idea of the range of ailments. It tastes like a mixture of anise and celery and grows wild where bears are found in the US, the Rocky Mountains, the southwestern states, and Mexico.

What ailments it helps
Congestion
Coughs
Flu
Sore throats
Wound healing

Which part to use
The brown root

How to consume it
Dried osha root can be cut and grated into smaller pieces and eaten. The herbalist Michael Moore advises eating a walnut-sized piece of root every 3-4 hours to ease symptoms.

A cold infusion is made by chopping 2-6 ounces of the root and adding boiling water. Allow this to cool and store in the refrigerator. Take a cup 3 times per day to ease symptoms. The cold-infusion mixture can also be used directly on wounds, as it is antiviral and antibacterial.

As cough syrup, make your own using a teaspoon of dried, grated osha added to 2 teaspoons of honey. Dilute the mixture with water and shake well.

In a commercial tincture, add 20 drops to water, and it is safe to take this 3-5 times daily or as advised by the label or a professional herbalist.

NOTES: Do not take osha if breastfeeding.

62. Passionflower
(Passiflora)

This gorgeous flower has over 500 varieties worldwide, but Native Americans used the nine species native to the US. When European settlers recognized the flower, their observation of Native American healing practices quickly became part of the general use of the plant in the US.

Flowering plants can be found from Ohio in the north, west to California, and south to the Florida Keys.

What ailments it helps
Anxiety
Depression
Epilepsy
Hyperactivity
Hysteria
Insomnia
Muscle pain
Seizures
Wound healing

Which parts to use
Leaves, roots, and fruit

How to consume it
Make a tea from the leaves and fresh, grated, or dried roots for any symptoms listed above.

Wounds: Wrap fresh leaves around wounds after cleaning them.

Make a poultice of leaves and apply for muscle pain.

Food source: The fruit is edible as passion fruit.

WARNING: Do not take this herb if pregnant or breastfeeding.

Peppermint
see Mint (PART 4)

63. Pinon / Pinyon Pine
(Pinus edulis)

This tree was significant to many Native American tribes. They used the tree so extensively that some described it as "the tree of life." The nuts were a trade item throughout the US and Canada for the Navajo, the Santa Clara tribes of New Mexico, the Hopi, and the Havasupai people. The Santa Clara tribe believes that the pinyon is the oldest tree of all trees. "It was an item of trade with the Hopi who live to the East" by the Havasupai. The Navajo chiefs are said to have bargained with General Sherman at Bosque Redondo in 1883, describing how these trees grew so many nuts that they could fill a wagon. The Navajo collect and sell the pinyon nuts to the people of the Hano Pueblo and the Jemez and Keresan Pueblos.

What ailments it helps
Abscesses
Boils
Colds
Coughs
Flu
Sores
Wound healing

Which parts to use
Young shoots and twigs, inner bark of mature wood, leaves, sap, pitch, and nuts

How to consume it
Inner bark: Make a decoction – see PART 7.

Pitch: Used to draw out the infected liquid from boils and abscesses by applying the pitch in a poultice.

Food: Nuts are edible as a food source. They are called pine nuts, pinyon nuts, and even "Indian nuts."

Leaves (needles) can be made into an infusion for colds/coughs as they are high in vitamin C.

Commercially produced pinyon pine oil is especially useful for respiratory health, either used in a diffuser or dropped in boiling water and inhaled.

64. (White) Pine
(Pinus strobus)

This tree is known as deal pine and soft pine and is native to North America. It can be found in areas of Newfoundland to the mountains in Georgia and central Iowa and west to parts of Illinois. Like the pinyon pine, the inner bark was used by Native Americans in decoctions, as well as young shoots, twigs, pitch, and leaves.

What ailments it helps
Abscesses
Arthritis
Boils

Bronchial infections
Headaches
Heartburn
Laryngitis
Painful joints
Whooping cough
Wound healing

Which parts to use
Young shoots and twigs, the inner bark of mature wood, pitch, and pine needles

How to consume it
Inner bark: Make a decoction – see PART 7. Use to ease the described ailments.

Pitch: Used to draw out the infected liquid from boils and abscesses by applying the pitch in a poultice like a pinyon pine. Poultices heal sores and cuts.

Infusion: Boil fresh or dried needles as per PART 7 to create pine needle tea. Drink for its pleasing taste, to help with pain, and for easing respiratory ailments.

65. Plantain
(Plantago major)

This edible plant had a unique use for Native Americans. Powdered plantain root was carried in case of a rattlesnake bite and applied. Worldwide, plantain provides treatments as an antiseptic and fever reducer. As one of the nine sacred herbs treasured by the Saxon people in Europe, it has a long history as a medicinal herb. The Cherokee would chew on a small piece of root to help with toothache.

What ailments it helps
Allergies
Antibacterial
Anti-venom treatment for snakebites
Asthma
Bronchitis
Emphysema
Fevers
Hay fever
Respiratory disorders
Sore eyes
Stops bleeding
Toothache

Which parts to use
Leaves, fruit (seed head), and roots

How to consume it
On a wound: Both leaves and seeds are antibacterial. Add some leaves to the wound to stop bleeding and promote healing. You can make an ointment in summer with fresh leaves for winter.

Toothache: Chew the leaves, then hold them over the sore tooth for pain relief.

High fever: Apply plantain leaves directly on the skin to cool a fever.

Infusion: Fresh leaves are best and can be dried relatively quickly for later use or bought commercially. Drink to soothe allergies and respiratory issues or to bathe sore eyes.

A decoction of leaves can be created and added to water.

66. Poke Root
(Phytolacca decandra / Phytolacca americana)

Approach this plant cautiously, and pay close attention to instructions regarding its use! This plant's root is poisonous if not treated and prepared carefully. The Delaware people called it pocon and used it as a stimulant for the heart, whereas it was utilized as a purgative in Virginia by Native American people. The root was dried to use as a method to treat hemorrhoids and skin parasites. In addition, ground root powder was helpful in poultices to aid wound healing.

What ailments it helps
Arthritis
Congestion
Hemorrhoids
Laryngitis
Mastitis
Mumps
Neuralgia
Pain relief
Rheumatism
Sore throat
Tonsillitis

Which parts to use
Berries, seeds, and roots (tiny amounts of the root must be cooked or treated and never taken fresh).

How to consume it
Foresters in the US Appalachian Mountains chew both seeds and berries as a remedy for arthritis right up to the present day.

The root is dug, cleaned, and dried all year round. It can be used as a tea or a tincture. The root can also be powdered and used topically on skin conditions.

Various throat conditions are said to benefit from the use of poke root in Native American tradition. Native American use involved using a poultice for treating skin problems and parasites.

Some midwives use it as a treatment for mastitis in lactating mothers, applied topically.

Pain symptoms are eased by cream, poultice, or ointment made from poke root.

Use tea made from berries for painful symptoms of arthritis, rheumatism, and the other painful ailments listed above.

Make an ointment from the dried and powdered root.

Take tea made from dried and powdered roots in very small amounts.

Make a tincture of fresh root. Chop a small amount and cover with alcohol as per PART 7.

NOTES: If making a tincture do NOT use this herb with the apple cider vinegar alternative!

It needs to steep in alcohol for six weeks, then strain and use a single drop at a time (a drop – not a dropper!) in water.

If in doubt, use proprietary root powder or tincture forms for peace of mind, and consult a professional herbalist.

67. Prickly Pear Cactus
(Opuntia engelmannii)

This plant has been hugely significant in Native American diets for centuries, demonstrated in archaeological finds. Eating raw pulp from this plant has improved blood sugar control and reduced cholesterol. The pads offer antiseptic and antibiotic properties to aid wound healing. They can also be used to help boils and to stop bleeding. In addition, the leaves were used to make moisturizers and sunscreen by Native Americans.

What ailments it helps
Antibiotic
Antiseptic
Boils
Diabetes
Lowers cholesterol
Prostate problems
Skin conditions
Stops bleeding
Urinary tract infections (UTIs)
Wound healing

Which part to use
Pads

How to consume it
The pulp reduces the rate of sugar absorption, so eating raw pulp can reduce symptoms of insulin shock.

Split pads are antiseptic and used for wounds. Make a poultice from pads and apply it to wounds. Split pads are used to stop bleeding.

Collect the moisture from pads and use it as a moisturizer and sunscreen.

A hot poultice of pad skin is applied to boils.

Make an infusion of the pads to treat swollen prostate and urinary infections.

Tea made from the pads is helpful with treating scar tissue.

68. Rabbit Tobacco
(Pseudognaphalium obtusifolium)

Also called Cherokee tobacco, sweet everlasting, and fragrant cudweed, this plant grows throughout eastern North America. It prefers dry, sandy soil, and can be seen thriving by the roadside and in the wasteland. Adventurous American youngsters used to "smoke" rabbit tobacco in corncob pipes, but it contains no nicotine and this activity rapidly lost popularity.

Native Americans believed the plant had spiritual powers. Cherokee and Lumbee Indians of North Carolina used it in sweat lodges and sweat baths. The Alabama used it for insomnia. Chewed leaves were rubbed on the bodies of some tribes for protection in battle. Others believed the smoke of rabbit tobacco would prevent bad luck.

In addition, modern herbal usage includes pain relief, as a sedative, and for diarrhea. Asthma, blocked sinuses, colds, coughs, sore throats, and other bronchial conditions are said to be helped by its use. It is also anti-viral. Skin sores and burns are aided with the use of a poultice. Rabbit tobacco should only be harvested in the fall and winter after the leaves are dry and have lost their color, or they will not have developed their true curative value. You don't want the seeds all over your house, so shake the harvested plant well in the field. The plant needs to remain outside for a few days to dry, then shake again before taking indoors. Also, beware of spiders, insects, and moth cocoons hiding within your harvested plant, as it's a favored habitat.

What ailments it helps

Asthma
Bronchial conditions
Colds and blocked sinuses
Coughs
Diarrhea
Insomnia
Skin sores and burns

Which parts to use

Leaves, once they have turned silvery brown – discard the flowers and stem.
Dried flowers for infusions.

How to consume it

Infusion of dried leaves or flowers – not too many leaves (3-4) as it can be quite bitter. Adding honey can help. A poultice of dried leaves for skin sores and burns. See PART 7.

Steam treatment for sinuses: Add a pinch of dried rabbit tobacco leaves to a cup of boiling water, cool slightly, and put into a humidifier. If you do not have one, place your head over a bowl, cover it with a towel to contain the steam, and inhale.

As a tincture, follow the recipe in PART 7 using the dried herb, and use a few drops to make tea.

69. Red Clover
(Trifolium pratense)

Colors range from red to pink/purple in this plant. Native Americans widely used red clover after its introduction by European settlers. They believed infusions of the leaves and flowers were helpful for whooping cough, cancer, and as an ointment for snakebites and other skin irritations. Eventually, tribes in California and Arizona used it as a food crop.

Today, the flowers of red clover are used to ease skin conditions and have also been investigated as an herbal aid in treating cancer, as native usage suggested. In addition, the flowers show a similar action to the female hormone estrogen and have been used as a hormone replacement therapy in menopausal women. The Blackfeet of Western Montana use red clover, amongst other herbs, to help ease the symptoms of Parkinson's Disease.

What ailments it helps

Bites and stings
Bronchitis
Conjunctivitis
Eczema
Fluid retention
Menopausal symptoms
Parkinson's Disease
Psoriasis
Respiratory infections
Treating cancers, particularly breast and ovarian cancer
Whooping cough

Which part to use
Fresh and dried flower heads

How to consume it
Tincture in water.

Infusions are made from flower heads. 1-3 teaspoons of dried flower heads to one cup of boiling water.

NOTES: Do not give red clover to children.

WARNING: Due to mimicking estrogen, avoid it if pregnant or breastfeeding.

Rose / Rosehip

see Wild Rose (93)

70. Rosemary

see PART 4

71. Sage

see PART 4

72. Saltbush

(Atriplex canescens)

Native Americans made extensive use of fourwing saltbush. Stems were used for fuel. Yellow dyes are made by boiling the leaves with raw alum. Saltbush seeds are edible (with a naturally mild, salty taste) and were ground into flour by the Navajo. The Paiute heated the leaves with water and treated sore muscles and general aches and pains. The Zuni made a healing ointment from fourwing saltbush for wound healing. This process involved chewing the flowers and roots in their mouths, and the saliva made a potion applied directly to stings and insect bites. The Paiute boiled the leaves and used the mixture to treat aches and sore muscles.

What ailments it helps
Bites and stings
Burns
Muscle aches
Wound healing

Which parts to use
Roots, leaves, flowers, and seeds

How to consume it

Roots and flowers are chewed, then the mixture is applied directly to insect bites.

Seeds are edible and can be made into flour. Leaves can be mixed with water, boiled, and fixed in poultices for wounds and burns.

Use the leftover water as a wash for aching muscles.

73. Sarsaparilla

(Smilax regelii, Smilax aspera)

Smilax Aspera Plant

Dried Sarsaparilla Root

This prickly, trailing vine is native to Central America and often used in soft drinks. It was introduced to European medicine by contact with the indigenous tribes of South America. In the sixteenth century, it was a treatment for syphilis, and the herb was exported from America around the world. Sarsaparilla is approved in the US for food use. The taste of sarsaparilla root is quite bitter, and other flavors, such as licorice or wintergreen, are typically added to make it palatable. This herb tastes like root beer, and the Council of Europe permits its use as a natural food coloring agent. Commission E approves it for psoriasis, rheumatic complaints, and also renal disease, used as a diuretic. In Central and South America it was traditionally used as treatment for impotence. Native Americans used to combine sweetgrass with sarsaparilla to make a drink to soothe coughs. The Penobscot were known to have used the dried powdered root for this purpose. A tea from the dried root was used for the common cold, skin diseases, and ringworm. Tests on rats concluded that the root had an anti-inflammatory and liver-protective effect.

What ailments it helps

Anti-inflammatory
Colds
Coughs
Fluid retention
Liver health
Male libido
Psoriasis
Rheumatism
Rheumatoid arthritis
Ringworm
Skin diseases

Which part to use

Roots

How to consume it

Tincture: Steep the root in alcohol to extract the active compounds. See how to make a tincture in PART 7.

Root infusion: Clean and dry the root tuber, then grate it to use in infusions. Use a teaspoon of grated herb, add a cup of boiling water, then strain and drink.

Taking this herb was popular as an aphrodisiac. Remedy coughs from the grated root, in an infusion.

NOTES: It's essential to limit taking excessive amounts of this herb.

WARNING: Do not take if pregnant.

If taking other medication orally, try to take sarsaparilla two hours before other medicines, and check the dosage with your professional herbalist.

When working with the root of the plant, the underground part (aka tubers), Jacob reminds us to ensure the plant has enough root left to grow back.

74. Sassafras

(Sassafras albidum)

These plants grow from Maine to Ontario and southern Texas. It was used as a food source and medicine by Native Americans so that when settlers arrived, they also began to use the plant, having seen its value. The Choctaw taught French settlers in Louisiana to dry and mash sassafras leaves, an essential natural thickener and ideal for stews, soups, or gumbos. It is still an oft-used ingredient in Cajun and Creole cooking.

What ailments it helps
Chickenpox
Colds
Fever
Flu
Measles

Which parts to use
Bark, leaves, and roots

How to consume it
Tincture: Native Americans used the bark and the roots for symptom relief of the listed ailments. Bark or root tincture is made by soaking parts in alcohol or vinegar – see PART 7.

Food: Leaves were used in food preparation as a thickener.

75. Saw Palmetto

(Serenoa repens)

Saw Palmetto Plant

Dried Berries

This shrub grows throughout South Carolina, Florida, and even across parts of Texas. It can grow to 10 feet (3.05 m) high, and berries appear between October to December.

Saw palmetto was used as a staple food for many Native American tribes. The berries were also used for medicinal purposes, mainly for men to treat prostate inflammation and excess urination at night, but also for infertility. Another use for this plant was its good foliage, which is used in basketry.

What ailments it helps
Nighttime incontinence
Prostate function
Sexual health (in men)

Which parts to use
Berries, fresh or dried, leaves, and branches

How to consume it
Berries: Make a tincture (see PART 7) or dry them in sunshine or an oven on low heat. It can be stored whole or ground into a powder and stored in a sterilized jar in a dark storage area.

Tea: Add two teaspoons of dried, whole berries to two cups of boiling water in a pan, then switch off and let steep with a lid on for 15 minutes. Add honey to taste, strain then drink.

The foliage was used for basketry.

NOTES: Jacob recommends herbal usage for men only.

76. Seneca Snakeroot
(Polygala senega)

Plant

Dried Root

This plant's root was chewed by Native Americans and applied directly in the event of a snakebite. It is also effective against other stings and bites. The roots were used to make a cough mixture, and today you can also make (or buy) a tincture. Snakeroot was used traditionally for heart complaints, but it may interfere with other heart medications, so check with your herbalist or medical practitioner before taking this plant.

What ailments it helps
Bites
Colds
Coughs
Heart complaints
Snakebites
Stings
Wound healing

Which part to use
Roots

How to consume it
Dig up part of the root, then dry, grate, or powder, and store – see PART 7 for guidance.

Use the powder to treat wounds.

Make a cough mixture.

Make a tincture.

NOTES: Check with your herbalist if you are taking other medications for any of the conditions listed above to find out how they may interact.

Michael Moore advises against its use if pregnant.

Shavegrass

see Horsetail (49)

---

77. Skullcap

(Scutellaria lateriflora)

Many Native American tribes used skullcap as a sedative and as tobacco. The plant grows in damp sites and has over 90 related species in various countries besides the US. However, American Skullcap is not the same plant as the Chinese Skullcap (Scutellaria baicalensis).

In the US, this herb is listed by the FDA as an herb of Undefined Safety. The herb is used ceremonially to induce visions by smoking it like tobacco. The unique shape of the flower gives it its name. It resembles a helmet, and this herb is called quaker bonnet and helmet flower.

Flowering generally occurs from May to August. Gardeners in southern areas enjoy the blooms which often appear in flower beds in drought-tolerant gardens. Pick leaves in summer when the plant flowers, dry the leaves in the shade, and store them for later use.

What ailments it helps
After birth, it is used to expel the placenta
Epilepsy
Headaches
Healthy menstrual cycles
Hysteria
Insomnia
Kidney health
Menstrual cramp relief
Nervousness
Neuralgia
Parkinson's Disease
Relieve withdrawal symptoms from prescribed medication such as barbiturates
Sedative
Sore throats
Stimulates the reproductive system after birth

Which parts to use
Leaves and roots

How to consume
Infusion of the root or leaves (fresh or dried) – see PART 7.

Decoction of the root.

Tincture drops in water to create a tonic, a few drops under the tongue.

WARNING: Avoid if pregnant as it may cause miscarriage.

78. Slippery Elm
(Ulmus rubra)

Native Americans use this tree in many traditional ways. They use the inner bark externally in poultices and internally in medicinal drinks. The Council of Europe lists slippery elm as a food flavoring. In addition, Native Americans used the inner bark to fashion bowstrings, rope, thread, and clothing.

What ailments it helps
Externally:
Abscesses
Boils
Burns
Gout
Rheumatism
Skin disorders
Swollen glands
Ulcers

Internally:
Colitis
Diarrhea
Fevers
Gastric and duodenal ulcers
Inflammation of the stomach
Sore throats
Stomach upsets
Toothaches

Which part to use
Inner bark: To remove some from the tree, make a small cut on the east side. Then cut a line with a sharp knife and peel back the outer bark in this area. Cut again to remove the inner bark. Do not cut from the same place again until the tree has healed.

How to consume it
Dry the bark, and then add it to poultices, tinctures, infusions, and ointment oils – see PART 7.

Make a tea: Use a teaspoon of powdered bark in a cup of boiling water, strain, and drink.

NOTES: Do not use the outer bark; it is known to cause miscarriages.

79. St. John's Wort
(Hypericum perforatum)

For Native Americans, this herb was a wound healer. Modern knowledge reveals that the active compound, hyperforin, is an excellent antibiotic. Today, treatment is often an ointment made from the aerial parts of the plant. This herb is also commonly used to combat depression and neuralgia.

What ailments it helps
Bruises
Cuts

Depression
General anxiety
Inflammation
Menopausal anxiety
Neuralgia
Psoriasis
Sciatica pain
Shingles
Sunburn
Varicose veins

Which parts to use
Leaves and flowers

How to consume it
Make a flower tea infusion and allow it to steep for 10 minutes; strain before drinking. Helpful for soothing the ailments listed.

Make herb oil or ointment using fresh flowers. Use this healing lotion and apply it topically on the skin for cuts, bruises, psoriasis, sunburn, and varicose veins. The flowers are completely edible and are often added to other foods like salads.

Make a tincture from fresh flowers and leaves.

See how to make infusions, herb oils, ointments, and tinctures in PART 7.

NOTES: Can cause sensitivity to light (photosensitivity).

Discontinue use if surgery is planned. Its use is not advised at the same time as surgery because it may interfere with other pharmaceuticals.

80. Stoneseed
(Lithospermum ruderale)

Western stoneseed is native to western parts of Canada and the United States, where its preferred habitat is mainly dry. In the right conditions, stoneseed plants grow up to a foot (30 cm) but cannot be grown in the shade. This plant is known to help give relief from rheumatic pain and kidney complaints. In addition, there is confirmed use by the Navajo and the Shoshone that they used it as a contraceptive.

What ailments it helps
Contraception
Diarrhea
Kidney complaints
Rheumatism

Which parts to use
Leaves, stems, and roots

How to consume it
Poultice: Use fresh or dried powdered leaves and stems in a poultice to ease rheumatism pain.

Infusion: Make a hot water infusion of powdered leaves and stems.

Decoction: Use fresh or dried roots - see PART 7.

Tincture: Check with a qualified practitioner.

WARNING: Estrous cycle elimination (contraception) – Please seek advice from an herbalist or professional medical practitioner before using this herb for contraception.

81. Sumac

see PART 4

82. Sweetgrass

(Hierochloe odorata)

This herb is one of the Four Sacred Medicines (see PART 2 for more details). Its use by Native American tribes was as a purifying herb in smudging ceremonies, where it was braided and burned. It is also said to purify the air spiritually and attract positive energy to a situation or problem. The Siksika Blackfoot tribe in the Great Plains used it as an infusion for colds. Using it in steam inhalation or a bath will bring relief from congestion. Like sage and cedar, sweetgrass is used to purify the home. It is used in smudging ceremonies to purify the sacred space. Also used in basketry and to make areas smell good due to the vanilla-infused scent of the herb. Stems soaked in water were then used as eyewash.

What ailments it helps

Chapped skin
Colds
Congestion
Eyewash
Hair tonic
Mosquito repellent

Which parts to use

Stems, all aerial parts, fresh and dried

How to consume it

Soak freshly picked herb stems and aerial parts in water and apply a poultice to ease tired eyes.

Make a tea from dried leaves to recover from colds.

Make an infusion with dried or fresh herbs to keep hair shiny, while the sweet smell of the meadow adds perfume to your hair.

Steam inhalation: Add fresh herb and a few drops of essential oil to boiling water in a basin, and cover with a towel. Place the head underneath the towel and inhale the steam to provide relief from colds.

Chapped skin: Add a few drops of herb oil to an ointment and rub in well, or make an infusion and apply this directly on the affected skin. It's also useful added to bathwater.

Adding a few drops of the sweetgrass herb oil to a candle burner helps repel insects.

To create oil – see PART 7.

Ceremonial use: Burn some fresh herbs in any space you want to purify.

83. Thyme
(Thymus vulgaris) and
Wild Mountain Thyme
(Thymus serpyllum)

Thymus Vulgaris

Thymus Serpyllum

As a cooking ingredient, this herb needs no introduction. In addition, it is widely used in medical and cosmetic products for its essential healing ingredient, thymol. It is known to be antiseptic and can be used directly on wounds if made into an essential oil or a healing ointment. Two types of thyme grow in the US: garden thyme and creeping thyme, also known as mountain thyme or wild thyme. Both varieties contain the same ingredient and can be used interchangeably. Health Canada approved the traditional uses of thyme (for throat and upper respiratory infections) and in ointments for minor skin irritations or wounds in 2008.

What ailments it helps
Antiseptic
Congestion
Nutrition
Pneumonia
Respiratory problems
Skin irritations
Sore throat
Wound healing

Which part to use
Leaves

How to consume it
To season food in casseroles, stews, and cooked soups, add thyme for a unique flavor.

Tea can be made for sore throats.

Thyme oil is added to wound ointment to promote healing or rubbed in directly. It is also recommended to rub it on the chest twice daily for pneumonia.

Make a healing ointment with thyme, mullein, and lavender to put on cuts and grazes to help prevent infection.

Add oil to bathwater or use fresh leaves, which make a relaxing aromatic bath, and the steam will help to relieve congestion.

Add fresh herb to boiled water in a basin. Cover with a towel and inhale the steam to ease nasal congestion.

84. Tobacco
(Nicotiana)

Tobacco is the first sacred medicine given to humanity by the Creator, and there are over sixty species that grow wild. Some are grown for their gorgeous scented flowers, which open in tubular bells when the sun starts to set. Natural tobacco, not the chemical-filled processed type, is used for smoking ceremonies and sweat lodges. Tribe members believed smoking tobacco was a way to access the spiritual world. When Columbus observed its use by Native Americans in the 15th century, tobacco was thought to have potential therapeutic properties to treat a variety of conditions.

What ailments it helps
Bites
Cuts
Earache
Insect and snakebites
Pain relief
Poison antidote
Skin conditions
Sores
Stops bleeding

Which part to use
Leaves, fresh or smoked

How to consume it
Make a poultice of leaves for pain relief and wound healing for sores and bites.

Tobacco is a ceremonial plant used to show gratitude in various settings, for example, when collecting parts of other plants (as described in PART 2).

Smoking: Tobacco is rolled and lit in traditional peace pipe ceremonies. Traditionally some tribes' usage included blowing the smoke into the ears to help with earache.

WARNING: Smoking anything at all should be avoided in pregnancy.

85. Uva Ursi
(Arctostaphylos)

This plant is known as bearberry or bear grape because bears like to eat the fruit. Native Americans used it medicinally for bladder and urinary tract infections. It has been effective in treating cystitis, diarrhea, problems with menstruation, hemorrhoids, and for aiding kidney problems. Externally, it can treat herpes and yeast infections, cold sores, cuts, and skin abrasions. It is used to make a natural remedy to help with itching, including on the scalps of young babies. The berry is a common ingredient in baby shampoos, mixed with herbs like mint and willow bark. Uva ursi is only for external use in children, and drinking tea may contain some ingredients best for adults only.

What ailments it helps
Bladder infections
Cold sores
Cuts
Cystitis
Diarrhea
Hemorrhoids
Herpes
Itchy skin and scalp
Kidney problems
Menstrual problems
Pancreatic problems
Urinary tract infections (UTIs)
Wound healing
Yeast infections

Which parts to use
Leaves, fresh or dry, and berries

How to consume it
An infusion can be made for baby rash, sores on the skin, or itchy adult rashes. Apply with a cotton swab. Drinking the infusion is for adults only.

Add to shampoo.

Wound ointment for these conditions can also be made to apply externally on cold sores and cuts.

NOTES: Infusion of leaves is for adults only. Do not let children consume this herb.

WARNING: Avoid if pregnant.

86. Valerian
(Valeriana officinalis, Valeriana edulis)

Plant

Flower With Root

Valerian has been classed as GRAS (Generally Recognized As Safe) for food use in the US. In some parts of the US, the plant is described as invasive. Humanity has utilized the root in medicine for centuries, dating back to the Greeks and Romans. In Germany, valerian has been approved for use as a mild sedative. It was invaluable for hysteria, intestinal colic, cramps, insomnia, restlessness, anxiety, as a muscle relaxant, gastrointestinal pain, and irritable bowel syndrome. The Blackfoot used valerian root in tea to reduce anxiety and promote good sleep.

What ailments it helps
Anxiety
Hyperactivity (in children)
Insomnia in adults
IBS (irritable bowel syndrome)
Muscle cramps

Which part to use
Roots

How to consume it
Roots can be dried and grated or used fresh.

As an infusion, soak a teaspoon of dried valerian root in hot water for 10 minutes, then strain before drinking. For insomnia, it is often combined with St. John's wort, hops, or passionflower.

As a tincture – see PART 7.

NOTES: Valerian should be stopped a few days before surgery as it may interact with other medications.

87. Western Skunk Cabbage
(Lysichiton americanus)

Because of its smell, Native Americans gave the skunk cabbage its name. However, the name is deceptive because the plant has been used as a natural remedy for burns, sore throats, and to ease swelling among Native Americans for centuries. It grows in swamps and wet woodlands in the Pacific Northwest. In times of famine, it was sometimes used as food. They enjoyed the spicy or peppery taste of the leaves. However, eating leaves is not recommended because they can irritate the stomach lining and are poisonous in large quantities. Native Americans used fresh leaves to wrap food, and it has been described as "Indian wax paper."

What ailments it helps
Burns
Skin conditions
Swelling
Wound healing

Which part to use
Leaves, fresh or dried

How to consume it
Make oil ointment from leaves soaked in oil, strained, and resoaked with the addition of fresh leaves. After the two soakings, strain and seal in a sterilized container.

Leaves are used topically as a wound poultice or powder.

Apply leaves directly on a burn, or shake the powder form and cover with gauze.

WARNING: Do not take orally because the leaves contain calcium oxalate crystals, an irritant in small quantities and poisonous in large doses.

88. White Willow
(Salix alba)

White Willow Tree

Dried Willow Bark

The benefits of willow bark go back thousands of years as a remedy for pain and to reduce inflammation. It contains salicin, which has antioxidant properties and appears to ease nerve pain. This pain-killing property is the ingredient in the most common over-the-counter drug, aspirin. In conditions like bursitis and tendonitis, where swelling is a problem, willow bark has effectively reduced inflammation. Native Americans recognized its ability to treat soreness and reduce fever. Some Native Americans burned willow stems and used the ashes to treat sore eyes. The Blackfoot used bark as a painkiller, and this use is reinforced by scientific evidence that salicin acts like the drug aspirin.

What ailments it helps
Arthritis
Bursitis
Fevers
Flu
Headaches
Immune system
Inflammatory pain
Rheumatism
Tendonitis
Toothache

Which parts to use
Bark and stems

How to consume it
Eye infections: Native Americans are known to have burned willow stems and used powdered ashes for eye infections. However, Jacob has not tried this, so he recommends caution.

Tea: Use small pieces of fresh bark or dry them and make them into a powdered form for later use. To make tea, add small amounts of bark (1 teaspoon) to boiling water and allow it to cool, then strain and drink. The Cherokee soothed fevers with teas made from dogwood, feverwort, and willow bark. Collect the inner bark and use dried or fresh. The tea can be drunk for pain.

Tincture: Use the bark to make willow bark tincture. You will need to extract the richness by steeping pieces of bark in vodka (or any suitable alcohol) – see PART 7 for details of how to make a tincture. It can be taken using a dropper bottle, adding drops of the mixture to some water.

WARNING: Avoid if nursing or pregnant.

89. Wild Black Cherry
(Prunus serotina)

Also known as chokecherry, this tree provides luscious black fruit after its gorgeous white, scented flowers first appear in spring. It is found from Canada to Arizona and New Mexico. Fall is the best time to collect the bark from young trees because the summer's growth will make it most potent. Native Americans used it to soothe and ease the pains of giving birth and for colds, coughs, and upper respiratory problems. The Cherokee also used it as a sedative.

What ailments it helps
Arthritis
Asthma
Bronchitis
Colds
Coughs
Diarrhea
Dysentery
Eye inflammation
Fevers
Flu
Labor pains
Loss of appetite
Lung conditions
Nerve tonic
Sedative
Sore throats
Whooping cough

Which parts to use
Bark and fruit

How to consume it
First, remove the outer bark on a small patch of the trunk using a sharp knife. Strip off the outer layer of the bark and remove some inner bark. Dry the inner bark in a shady place, out of direct sunlight. Use the dried bark in tea and syrup.

Tea: Make tea from the dried bark and consume it warm. You can save excess in the refrigerator and reheat it when needed. Taking the tea may also cause drowsiness, so ensure you take it before sleep, not during activity.

Food: Eat the fruit raw, or make preserves or jelly.

Sedative mix: Prepare as a sedative, mixing hops, wild lettuce, and wild black cherry.

Syrup: Can be given as a tonic for sore throats, colds, and fevers. To make it, add 2 teaspoons (5 g) dried inner bark to 2 cups (0.47 l) of warm water. Allow this to simmer gently for an hour, then strain into a sterilized jar. Add some sugar or honey to taste sweeter if you prefer.

The Meskwaki tribe made a liquid from cherries, which they allowed to ferment for a year, and drank the juice to ease the symptoms of dysentery.

Cherry tonic wine: Use 2 cups (0.47 l) of ripe cherries, 2 cups (0.47 l) of sugar, and 2 cups (0.47 l) of water. Destone the fruit and add it to the sugar. Use boiling water to melt the sugar and allow the mixture to settle. Use a demijohn if you have one, as the liquid will begin to ferment, and you want to keep fruit flies away, or you will have cherry vinegar. When the liquid clears, strain into clean, clear bottles, and store them until needed.

NOTES: Be careful when using leaves or seeds of wild cherry, as they contain amygdalin. This chemical compound is toxic. Unfortunately, cherry stones also have this chemical, but luckily, we do not eat the seeds!

Cherry bark contains prussic acid, which is dangerous when consumed in high quantities. In addition, it is not recommended for use in people with liver or kidney problems.

90. Wild Carrot

(Daucus carota)

Originally native to Europe, the flowering wild carrot plant is now naturalized in northeast America and is also known as Queen Anne's lace. Not to be confused with the common carrot, whose roots we use for food, the wild carrot roots cannot be consumed unless from a very young plant. Modern wild carrots used for herbal remedies usually involve the parts that grow above the ground and oil from its seeds. Traditional Native American practice included chewing the plant's above-ground parts and applying them to snakebites. In addition, the Navajo and Nez Perce used raw and boiled roots rubbed onto the skin to help soothe irritations.

Wild carrot is used commercially in food, beverages, soaps, and lotions.

What ailments it helps

Cystitis
Diabetes
Digestive problems
Induce menstruation
Kidney stones
Skin irritations
Snakebites
Urinary tract problems (UTIs)

Which parts to use

Flowers, seeds, leaves, and roots

How to consume it

Tea: The Mohegan people made an infusion of flowers to make tea for diabetics.

Traditional Native American practice included chewing the plant's above-ground parts and applying them to snakebites.

Raw and boiled roots are rubbed onto the skin to help soothe irritations.

Infusions: Flowers and leaves can be made into infusions. However, the wild carrot seed oil is best purchased commercially.

WARNING: Avoid if pregnant, may cause miscarriage.

91. Wild Ginger
(Asarum canadense)

Not to be confused with root ginger, Native American usage of wild ginger is discussed in detail. The leaves of wild ginger grow in heart shapes, and the bell-shaped flowers offer a delicate color in any shady part of your garden. Testing has shown that the leaves of wild ginger contain two antibiotic compounds and are known to have been used in poultices by both Native Americans and newly arrived settlers to treat wounds.

What ailments it helps
Antibiotic
Appetite stimulant
Arthritis
Breast soreness
Colds
Coughs
Digestive issues
Earache
Fevers
Headaches
Scarlet Fever
Spasms
Vertigo
Wound healing

Which parts to use
Leaves and roots

How to consume it
Leaves can be picked fresh and applied to a wound as a poultice, fixed in place with gauze.

Leaves are dried, ground into powder, and added to an ointment for use in healing.

Roots are dug, dried, and ground into powder for wound use.

Roots can also be candied for decoration or used in small quantities as a spice in cooking for a mild ginger flavor. The Cherokee boiled the roots to make tea for coughs, colds, etc.

NOTES: There is a traditional use of wild ginger leaves being consumed as a spice (dried and used in cooking). However, they contain compounds under investigation at the time of this publication, so use them cautiously and sparingly. Handling the leaves may cause dermatitis in some people.

92. Wild Lettuce
(Lactuca virosa)

Wild lettuce is closely related to the lettuce we eat in green salads, and some varieties growing wild in the US have prickly leaves or taste bitter; these are often called bitter lettuce. The Cherokee were known to use this plant to make a sedative, as all these plants contain lactucarium, an ingredient that acts similarly to opium. When the leaves and stems are cut, you will notice a milky sap exuding from the cut. The sap is used to make medicine to soothe anxiety, ease whooping cough, and for problems with the kidneys. This plant offers a way to relieve the body naturally for excitable youngsters and people with insomnia.

What ailments it helps
Anxiety
Asthma
Coughs
Insomnia
Kidney problems
Restlessness
Whooping cough

Which parts to use
Leaves, stems, and seeds

How to consume it
Food: Green leaves can be added to salads.

Oil: Seeds can be harvested and ground into the oil. Use like wheat germ or olive oil.

Infusion: To make a mild sedative, mix leaves with hops – see PART 7.

Tincture: Add drops of the tincture to water and drink when needed – see PART 7.

Wild Mountain Thyme
see Thyme (83)

93. Wild Rose
(Rosa acicularis)

In Flower

With Rosehips

Most people recognize the fruit of the wild rose, commonly seen in hedgerows in the countryside. The sweet-smelling blooms transform into red rosehips by fall, and the names by which this plant is known refer to these colorful fruits: hip fruit, brier hip, sweetbriar, and briar rose. These shrubs can grow quite big, ranging from 3-9 feet (approx. 1-3 m) tall. Native American use of this shrub included infusions made from flower petals, eating the hips for a rich dose of vitamin C, and making tea from them as a diuretic. A Cherokee recipe for diarrhea used a decoction of the roots.

What ailments it helps
Colds
Coughs
Diarrhea
Diuretic

Fevers
Gout
Scurvy
Sore throats
Tired or sore eyes
Vitamin C deficiency

Which parts to use
Flower petals, fruit (rosehips), and roots

How to consume it
An infusion of flowers can be cooled and used to bathe sore or tired eyes. Make a decoction of the roots for diarrhea.

Make an infusion of rosehips to soothe sore throats.

It is a natural daily tea. Rosehips can be dried, made into rosehip syrup, and used in rosehip tea. A fantastic source of vitamin C, the fruit (rosehips) provides a daily vitamin boost taken as a tea or syrup.

Rosehip tea: You can dry rosehips collected for future use or stew the whole fresh or dried rosehips in warm water for 10 minutes, then strain and serve. Do not cut open the hips because they contain some scratchy black hairs inside, and it is important not to consume these, or they will irritate your throat, not soothe it! Using the entire rosehip gives you the stewed goodness without the black hairs. Therefore, it is still essential to double strain the liquid through a muslin cloth and then discard any black hairs that may have escaped the fruit.

Rosehip syrup: Make your own by picking rosehips in the fall. Try to harvest from areas where you know that no pesticides have been used. If you have space in a garden, you can control this by growing your own.

Root decoction – see PART 7 for how to prepare this.

NOTES: Collect rosehips from May onwards. Remember, if you have previously picked all the petals, there may be no rosehips later in the year. Dry picked rosebuds and save them in a dark bottle for winter.

The red fruit is visible on the bush from October onwards. Jacob says to pick after the first frosts, which are supposed to sweeten the fruit, which is incredibly rich in vitamin C. In addition, if you compare it pound for pound with oranges, it contains 20% more vitamin C.

94. Wild Yam
(Dioscorea villosa)

Wild Yam Root

For centuries, folk medicine used wild yams for various women's needs. As a contraceptive, ingestion of the herb appears to mimic the role of progesterone, one of the female hormones preventing pregnancy.

Native Americans made wild yam tea to relieve labor pains. In addition, it is said to ease the side effects faced by many going through postmenopausal symptoms. Also known as rheumatism root, this plant is used in pharmaceutical preparations to provide cortisone for painful joints and anabolic hormones that promote growth.

What ailments it helps
Arthritis
Contraceptive
Gallbladder pain
Labor pains
Pain and inflammation of joints
Painful periods
Postmenopausal symptoms
Rheumatism

Which part to use
Roots, fresh and dried

How to consume it
As an infusion in tea.

NOTES: In large quantities, it can cause oily skin. Anybody with cancer should avoid this plant.

WARNING: Avoid if pregnant, as it may affect the baby (male features such as body hair) except during active labor.

95. Witch Hazel
(Hamamelis virginiana)

This shrub grows wild in many areas in the US, from the south in Florida and Texas and northwards as far as Nova Scotia in Canada. An astringent is produced from the leaves and bark of the North American witch hazel shrub. It was a popular resource for medicinal purposes by Native Americans in the US and the people of Europe and Asia. It has delicate yellow hanging flowers, but it is mainly the witch hazel twigs that are used medicinally. The Potawatomi tribe made use of the twigs to relieve bruises and swelling and also to stop bleeding. Witch hazel is used worldwide to ease muscle aches and pain. Menominee warriors used a decoction of leaves before important games and dances and applied it directly to the legs of tribe members.

What ailments it helps
Acne
Bruises
Cracked or blistered skin
Eczema
Hemorrhoids
Ingrown nails
Muscle aches and pain
Psoriasis
Skin rashes
Stops bleeding
Sunburn
Swelling
Varicose veins

Which parts to use
Twigs, leaves, and bark

How to consume it
Decoction: The boiled twigs were used to make a decoction to cure external ailments. It is applied topically to the affected area. Leaves and bark also are made into a decoction – see PART 7.

Steam treatment: Derived by placing the twigs in water with hot rocks, it was a favorite Potawatomi treatment for muscle aches. Early Puritan settlers in New England adopted this remedy from the natives, and its use became widely established in the United States.

96. Wormwood

(Artemisia campestris, Artemisia absinthium)

Artemisia absinthium

This plant is also known as absinthe and green ginger. Leaves and flowering tops were gathered and dried for use. Historically, there are claims that it eases bronchial problems, including tuberculosis. For stomach problems, leaves were chewed to soothe the discomfort. In addition, a root infusion was applied externally for scalp irritations. Finally, a poultice of fresh leaves or flowers was made to cover and ease sore eyes.

What ailments it helps

Abortifacient (not to be used during pregnancy)
Bronchitis
Indigestion
Intestinal worms
Labor pains (only used when a baby was due)
Loss of appetite
Scalp irritations
Sore eyes
Stomach problems

Which parts to use

Leaves and flowers

How to consume it

Tea: Eases chest congestion.

Infusion: Use leaves and flowers in boiling water.

Poultice: Cover sore eyes.

WARNING: As there are claims that some Native American tribes used this herb to end difficult pregnancies, Jacob advises avoiding the use of wormwood for pregnant women. Seek professional medical advice.

97. Yarrow

see PART 4

98. Yellow Dock

(Rumex crispus)

Plant

Root

This plant is well-known for its ability to soothe nettle stings, and Native Americans used this plant as both food and medicine. The Navajo regarded this plant as a tonic, calling it a "Life

Medicine." The Cherokee would eat it in springtime as salad greens, but also made a hand wash from a decoction of the roots. It is a disinfectant and a method to treat skin rashes and sores, including diaper rash. This irritation is the body's attempt to remove toxins via the skin, and dock will remedy that. Its use in the past for ringworm is documented, but it is more commonly utilized to ease joint pain, and as food, it eases stomach aches. In addition, it has often been used to treat anemia because consumption of dock permits the body to absorb iron and other minerals easily.

What ailments it helps
Acne
Anemia
Constipation
Eczema
Joint pain
Rashes
Ringworm
Skin irritations
Stomach aches

Which part to use
Roots

How to consume it
Root tincture: Start with a small dose (1 ml once a day) and gradually increase the dosage to a maximum of 3 ml per day.

Food: Ability to allow the body to absorb iron and minerals from foods.

Tonic: Used daily as a healthy medicine for life.

Decoction: When used externally as a disinfectant, it removes toxins from the skin.

NOTES: Large amounts may cause sedative and diuretic effects.

WARNING: Avoid if pregnant.

99. Yerba Santa / Mountain Balm
(Eriodictyon californicum)

Plant

Dried Leaves

This herb was listed in the US Pharmacopeia in 1894. Spanish settlers named it yerba santa (sacred herb) after watching Native Americans use it. It was beneficial for all types of respiratory conditions, as well as for bruises, sprains, and any inflammatory disorders, e.g., joint pain.

Its pleasant flavor has resulted in its inclusion in commercially-prepared food and beverages and to mask the bitter taste in certain pharmaceutical drugs.

What ailments it helps
Asthma
Bronchitis
Bruises
Colds

Coughs
Inflammation
Joint pain
Sprains

Which part to use
Leaves

How to consume it
First aid: A poultice of leaves was applied to ease soreness and sprains. Before plasters and bandages replaced them, the leaves were used as they were sticky and could wrap around wounds to seal them.

Bruises: Make a poultice of the leaves and use it on the affected part. Change fresh leaves daily until the bruise improves. Leaves can be fixed with the natural stickiness of the plant or sealed with gauze over the leaves.

Tea: Use an infusion of leaves (fresh or dried) to help soothe pain or respiratory problems.

100. Yew: Pacific or Western Yew *(Taxus brevifolia)* and American or Canadian Yew *(Taxus canadensis)*

Yew is a perennial evergreen tree that grows widely in the US. However, it is known to be an extremely poisonous plant. Take extreme care when near yew trees with children so that they do not consume the tasty-looking berries, which provide birds with winter food. Due to its growing location, the Pacific yew's history for medicinal use was part of Native American culture, namely in the form of a bark decoction used to treat cancer. The Bella Coola and the Quinault people used dried bark to make lung medicine. Western medicine didn't recognize its vital uses until the 1960s.

What ailments it helps
Arthritis
Cancer
Fever
Rheumatism

Which parts to use
Bough tips and bark

How to consume it
For cancer treatment: In tests, the yew has shown to be effective in lung, ovarian, and breast cancer and is used in pharmaceutical treatments for these diseases. Because the pseudoalkaloids of various species of this plant provide antimitotic agents, they may help reduce the growth of cancerous cells. In addition, the taxol molecules have very limited solubility and need to be administered in ethanol and polyethoxylated castor oil. Please consult a professional medical practitioner for more information.

NOTES: Jacob emphasizes that yew is poisonous and should only be used with advice and supervision from a skilled herbalist or medical practitioner, so seek professional advice.

101. Yucca
(Yucca elata Engelmann)

This spiky, succulent plant grows tall in the wild in semi-desert land in the southern states of the US and Mexico. Its flowers are edible, even if you have to take great care not to get spiked by the leaves! It is a stately plant with large leaves arching into the air and has a tall stem of white flowers adored by bees. Native Americans used this plant to treat arthritis, inflammation, and joint pain. The sap from leaves can be applied in poultices, and the thick spiky leaves were shaped into belts, ropes, footwear, and woven into baskets. The Zuni used yucca as a hair wash for newborns to encourage hair growth.

What ailments it helps
Arthritis
Diabetes
Gallbladder problems
Headaches (migraine)
High blood pressure
Inflammation
Joint pain
Liver problems
Osteoarthritis
Pain relief
Sprains
Stops bleeding
Swelling
Wound healing

Which parts to use
Roots, sap, fruit, and flowers

How to consume it
Make a poultice: The sap can be applied directly in poultices for bleeding, sprains, inflammation, and wounds. The sap from the plant can be collected and applied directly – see PART 7.

Dig up a portion of the root to soak, crush it, and make it into a gentle shampoo.

Yucca can also be purchased in capsules for higher strength in treatments for arthritis.

Food: Edible yucca fruit grows on the thick-leaved varieties of yucca, and you need to pick the fruit from the flower when it is young, measuring about 4 inches (0.1 m) long. Eat raw or cooked. However, its taste is sweetened even more when cooked in a hot oven.

NOTES: The roots of one variety of yucca (Yucca constricta - Buckley's yucca) should not be consumed because they contain saponins, which may cause allergic reactions in some people. Best to avoid them.

Herbs to avoid in pregnancy
(See notes in individual herb listing.)

NOTE: Check with a medical professional before using any herbal remedy, especially if nursing or pregnant.

Angelica
Arnica
Bearberry
Black Cohosh
Blue Cohosh
Boswellia
Burdock
California Poppy
Cat's Claw
Cedar
Chasteberry
Chickweed
Damiana
Devil's Claw
Feverfew
(American) Ginseng
Goldenseal
Horsemint
Juniper
Passionflower
Red Clover
Rosemary (oil)
Sarsaparilla
Seneca Snakeroot
Skullcap
Slippery Elm (bark)
Tobacco
Uva Ursi
White Willow
Wild Carrot
Wild Yam
Wormwood
Yarrow
Yellow Dock

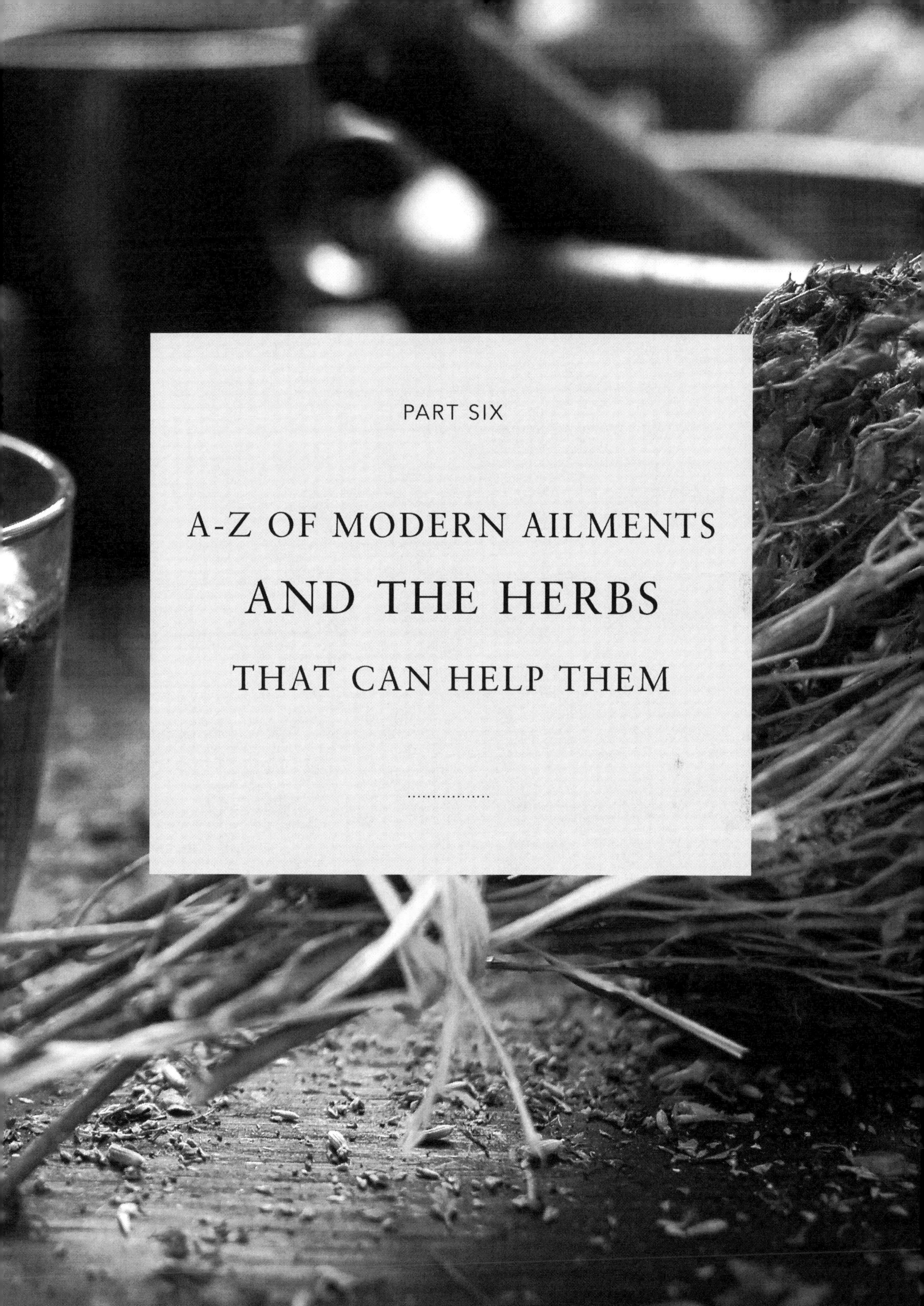

PART SIX

A-Z OF MODERN AILMENTS AND THE HERBS THAT CAN HELP THEM

See detailed notes on specific herb usage in PART 5

Disclaimer

These statements have not been evaluated by the Food and Drug Administration and Jacob makes no medical claims, nor intends to diagnose, treat, or heal medical conditions.

Women who are nursing or pregnant, or persons with known medical conditions, should consult their physician before taking any herbal products.

The use of herbal remedies for babies and children should always be approached cautiously, and consulting with your doctor is advised.

Always check for interaction with prescribed medications. Mixing natural and prescribed treatments is not always the best course of action.

NOTES: *Indicates you should avoid if pregnant or nursing.

A

Abscesses
Burdock*
Devil's Claw*
Echinacea
Lemon Balm
Pinon / Pinyon Pine
(White) Pine
Poke Root
Slippery Elm*

Aches
Boneset
Dandelion
Gentiana
Osha
(White) Pine
Saltbush
Wild Black Cherry
Wild Ginger

Acne
Buffaloberry
Burdock*
Cedar*
Chasteberry*
(Desert) Lavender
Red Clover*
Sarsaparilla*
Witch Hazel
Yarrow*
Yellow Dock*

ADHD
Oats
(Desert) Lavender
Skullcap*
St. John's Wort

Allergies
Angelica*
Goldenrod
Mint
Plantain

Amenorrhea – see **Menstrual Problems**

Anemia
Angelica*
Yellow Dock*

Antiseptic
Goldenrod
Pinon / Pinyon Pine
Prickly Pear Cactus
Sage
Sumac
Thyme

Anxiety
Damiana*
Hops
(Desert) Lavender
Lemon Balm
Mint
Passionflower*
Skullcap*
St. John's Wort
Valerian
Wild Lettuce

Aphrodisiac
Damiana*

Appetite Stimulant
Angelica*
Cedar*
Centaury
Damiana*
Dogwood
Garlic / Wild Garlic
Gentiana
(American) Ginseng*
Sage
Wild Black Cherry
Wild Ginger
Wormwood*

Arthritis
Aloe Vera
Black Cohosh*
Boneset
Boswellia*
Buffaloberry
Cat's Claw*
Devil's Claw*
Horsemint*
Horsetail

Juniper*
Oregon Grape
(White) Pine
Poke Root
Sarsaparilla*
Slippery Elm*
Stoneseed
White Willow*
Wild Black Cherry
Wild Ginger
Wild Yam*
Yellow Dock*
Yucca

Asthma
Black Haw
Boswellia*
Cedar*
Coltsfoot
Damiana*
Evening Primrose
Garlic / Wild Garlic
Goldenrod
Honeysuckle
Mullein
Plantain
Rabbit Tobacco
Wild Black Cherry
Wild Lettuce
Yerba Santa / Mountain Balm
Yew

Astringent
Goldenrod
Sumac
Wild Rose (hips)
Witch Hazel
Yarrow*

B

Backache
Arnica*
Devil's Claw*
Feverwort
Gentiana
Horsemint*

Bites – see **Insect Bites and Stings**

Bladder problems
Borage
Cleavers
Goldenrod
Horsetail
Oak
Stoneseed
Uva Ursi*
Wild Carrot*
Wild Rose

Bleeding (to control)
Goldenrod
Hemlock (native)
Horsetail
(Desert) Lavender
Nettle
Oregon Grape
Plantain
Prickly Pear Cactus
Witch Hazel
Yarrow*

Bloating
Lemon Balm

Blood Pressure (to lower)
Black Haw
Damiana*
Garlic / Wild Garlic
Hawthorn
Sumac
Yucca

Blood Vessels – see **Circulatory Health**

Boils
Borage
Buffaloberry
Burdock*
Cattail
Chamomile
Devil's Claw*
(American) Ginseng*
Goldenrod
Hops
Pinon / Pinyon Pine
(White) Pine
Prickly Pear Cactus
Slippery Elm*
Tobacco*

Bowel Complaints – see **Constipation** or **Diarrhea**

Breast Milk (to increase flow)
Garlic / Wild Garlic
Nettle

Breast Milk (to stop flow)
Sage

Breast Soreness
Chasteberry*
Wild Ginger

Broken Bones
Boneset
Comfrey
Nettle

Bronchial Infections / Problems
Angelica*
Cedar*
Coltsfoot
Echinacea
Elderflower
Garlic / Wild Garlic
Horsemint*
Mint
Mullein
(White) Pine
Plantain
Rabbit Tobacco
Red Clover*
Wild Black Cherry
Wormwood*
Yerba Santa / Mountain Balm

Bruises
Arnica*
Borage
Comfrey
St. John's Wort
Witch Hazel

Burns
Aloe Vera
Cattail
Coltsfoot
(American) Feverfew
Horsetail
(Desert) Lavender
Oak
Pinon / Pinyon Pine

Prickly Pear Cactus
Rabbit Tobacco
Saltbush
Slippery Elm*
Western Skunk Cabbage

C

Canker Sores – see **Gum and Mouth Problems**

Cancer
Boswellia*
Goldenseal*
Oats
Red Clover*
Yew

Cardiac Health – see **Heart Health**

Catarrh – see **Congestion**

Chickenpox Symptoms
Sassafras

Childbirth
Nettle
Wild Black Cherry
Wild Yam*
Wormwood*

Induce Labor
Wild Carrot*

To Speed Childbirth
Black Cohosh*
Blue Cohosh*

To Speed Delivery of the Placenta
Skullcap*

To Stop Postpartum Difficulties
Angelica*
Skullcap*

To Relieve the Pain of Childbirth
Blue Cohosh*
Wild Black Cherry
Wild Yam*
Wormwood*

Cholesterol (to lower)
Flaxseed
Garlic / Wild Garlic
Oats
Prickly Pear Cactus
Sumac

Circulatory Health & Problems
Angelica*
Dandelion
Plantain
Yarrow*
Yellow Dock*

Colds
Blackberry
Boneset
Broom Snakeweed
Dogwood
Echinacea
Elderflower
Garlic / Wild Garlic
Goldenrod
Hemlock (native)
Honeysuckle
Horsemint*
Juniper*
(Desert) Lavender
Mullein
Mint
Osha
Pinon / Pinyon Pine
Rabbit Tobacco
Sarsaparilla*
Sassafras
Seneca Snakeroot*
Sumac
Sweetgrass
Wild Black Cherry
Wild Ginger
Yarrow*
Yerba Santa / Mountain Balm

Cold Sores – see **Gum and Mouth Problems**

Congestion
Angelica*
Buckbrush
Goldenrod
Horsemint*
Osha
Poke Root
Mint
Mullein
Rabbit Tobacco
Sweetgrass
Thyme

Conjunctivitis – see **Eye Problems**

Constipation
Aloe Vera
Broom Snakeweed
Elderflower
(American) Ginseng*
Oats
Yellow Dock*

PLEASE NOTE TAKING HIGH FIBER FOODS INCLUDING FRUIT AND VEGETABLES MAY BE THE BEST WAY TO CONTROL THIS.

Convalescence After Illness or Injury
(American) Ginseng*
Oak

Contraceptives
Stoneseed
Wild Yam*

Convulsions
Wild Ginger

Coughs
Angelica*
Blackberry
Blue Cohosh*
Boneset
Borage
Broom Snakeweed
Burdock*
Chickweed*
Coltsfoot
Echinacea
Elderflower
Flaxseed
Hemlock (native)
Honeysuckle
(Desert) Lavender
Mullein
Osha
Pinon / Pinyon Pine
Plantain
Rabbit Tobacco
Sarsaparilla*
Wild Black Cherry

Wild Ginger
Wild Lettuce
Wild Rose
Yerba Santa / Mountain Balm

Cramps (also see **Muscle Problems**)
Blue Cohosh*
Chamomile
(American) Ginseng*
Valerian

Cuts
Aloe Vera
Buffaloberry
Goldenrod
Pinon / Pinyon Pine
(White) Pine
St. John's Wort
Uva Ursi*
Witch Hazel

Cystitis
Buckbrush
Uva Ursi*
Wild Carrot*

D

Dandruff and Scalp Irritations
Burdock*
Uva Ursi*
Wormwood*

Depression
Boswellia*
Damiana*
Passionflower*
St. John's Wort

Detox – see **Toxins**

Diabetes
Blackberry
Oats
Prickly Pear Cactus
Wild Carrot*
Yucca

Diaphoretic (**sweat-promoter**)
Burdock*
Pinon / Pinyon Pine

Diarrhea
Blackberry
Borage
Dogwood
Feverwort
Garlic / Wild Garlic
Gravel Root / Joe Pye Weed
Hemlock (native)
Mint
Oak
Rabbit Tobacco
Slippery Elm*
Stoneseed
Uva Ursi*
Wild Black Cherry
Wild Rose

Digestive Disorders, Conditions, and General Health
Blackberry
Damiana*
Dogwood
Gentiana
(American) Ginseng*
Goldenseal*
Honeysuckle
Horsemint*
Juniper*
Lemon Balm
Mint
Oats
Rosemary*
Sage
Slippery Elm*
Wild Carrot*
Wild Ginger
Wild Rose
Wormwood*

Diuretic (also see **Fluid Retention**)
Angelica*
Blue Cohosh*
Burdock*
Cleavers
Dandelion
Elderflower
(American) Feverfew
Gravel Root / Joe Pye Weed
Horsemint*
Horsetail
Juniper*
Sarsaparilla*
Saw Palmetto
Wild Rose

Dropsy – see **Fluid Retention**

Dysmennorrhea – see **Menstrual Cramps**

Dyspepsia – see **Indigestion**

E

Earache and Ear Infections
Chamomile
(American) Ginseng*
Mullein
Wild Ginger

Eczema
Borage
Burdock*
Coltsfoot
Red Clover*
Witch Hazel
Yellow Dock*

Emphysema
Garlic / Wild Garlic
Plantain

Endometriosis
Chasteberry*

Energy / Exhaustion
Damiana*
(American) Ginseng*
Oats

Epilepsy
Blue Cohosh*
Chasteberry*
Passionflower*
Skullcap*
Wild Carrot*

Eye Problems, Irritation, Soreness
Buffaloberry
Chickweed*
Dandelion
Elderflower
Goldenseal*
Plantain
Red Clover*
Sweetgrass
Wild Black Cherry
Wild Rose

White Willow*
Wormwood*

F

Fatigue
Cat's Claw*
(American) Ginseng*
(Desert) Lavender
Oats

Fertility
Blue Cohosh*
(American) Ginseng*
Saw Palmetto

Fevers
Boneset
Broom Snakeweed
Buckbrush
Coltsfoot
Dandelion
Dogwood
Evening Primrose
(American) Feverfew
Feverfew*
Feverwort
Gentiana
(American) Ginseng*
Goldenrod
Gravel Root / Joe Pye Weed
Hemlock (native)
Honeysuckle
Horsemint*
Mint
Osha
Plantain
Sassafras
Slippery Elm*
Sumac
White Willow*
Wild Black Cherry
Wild Ginger
Wild Rose
Yew

Fibroids
Chasteberry*

Flatulence
Cedar*
Horsemint*
Lemon Balm
Mint
Sage
Wild Carrot*

Flu
Boneset
Chamomile
Coltsfoot
Echinacea
Elderflower
Feverwort
(American) Ginseng*
Goldenrod
Goldenseal*
Hemlock (native)
(Desert) Lavender
Mint
Mullein
Nettle
Osha
Pinon / Pinyon Pine
(White) Pine
Rabbit Tobacco
Sassafras
White Willow*
Wild Black Cherry
Yarrow*

Fluid Retention
Angelica*
Blue Cohosh*
Burdock*
Cedar*
Cleavers
(American) Feverfew
Gravel Root / Joe Pye Weed
Horsemint*
Horsetail
Juniper*
Red Clover*
Sarsaparilla*
Wild Lettuce

G

Gallbladder Problems
Burdock*
Dandelion
Wild Yam*
Yucca

Gallstones
Buffaloberry

Gastrointestinal Complaints and Ulcers
(Desert) Lavender
Mint
Oregon Grape
Slippery Elm*
Valerian
Wormwood*

Gonorrhea
Cleavers
Dogwood

Gout
Burdock*
Chickweed*
Devil's Claw*
Goldenrod
Horsetail
Gravel Root / Joe Pye Weed
Slippery Elm*
Wild Rose

Gum and Mouth Problems
Blackberry
Buckbrush
Echinacea
Goldenseal*
Hawthorn
Lemon Balm
Sage
Uva Ursi*

H

Hair Health, Loss
Aloe Vera
Burdock*
Nettle
Sweetgrass
Uva Ursi*
Yucca

Hay Fever
Chamomile
Plantain
Yarrow*

Headache (including Migraine)
Angelica*
Black Cohosh*
Boneset
Broom Snakeweed
California Poppy*

Devil's Claw*
Dogwood
(American) Feverfew
Feverfew*
Gentiana
(American) Ginseng*
Lemon Balm
Mint
(White) Pine
Skullcap*
White Willow*
Wild Ginger
Yucca

Heart and Circulatory Health & Problems
Flaxseed
Hawthorn
Prickly Pear Cactus
Red Clover*
Seneca Snakeroot*

Heartburn
Centaury
Dandelion
Juniper*
(Desert) Lavender
Mint
(White) Pine
Wormwood*

Hemorrhages – see **Bleeding**

Hemorrhoids
Buckbrush
Chamomile
Poke Root
Witch Hazel
Yarrow*

Herpes
Uva Ursi*

Hiccups
Blue Cohosh*
Chamomile
Mint

Hyperactivity
California Poppy*
Passionflower*
St. John's Wort
Valerian

Hysteria
Passionflower*
Skullcap*
Valerian

I

Immune System (strengthen)
Cat's Claw*
Prickly Pear Cactus

Impotence
Damiana*
Sarsaparilla*

Incontinence
Saw Palmetto

Indigestion
Angelica*
Borage
Centaury
Hawthorn
Horsemint*
Juniper*
Lemon Balm

Infections
Cattail
Echinacea
Goldenseal*

Inflamed Nasal Passages
Echinacea
Yellow Dock*

Inflammation / Swelling
Aloe Vera
Arnica*
Blackberry
Boswellia*
Buckbrush
Buffaloberry
Cat's Claw*
Cattail
Chamomile
Chasteberry*
Chickweed*
Dandelion
Devil's Claw*
Echinacea
Elderflower
Gentiana
(American) Ginseng*
Hops
Horsemint*
Juniper*
Mullein
Oak
(White) Pine
Poke Root
Skullcap*
St. John's Wort
Western Skunk Cabbage
White Willow*
Wild Black Cherry
Wild Yam*
Witch Hazel
Yarrow*
Yerba Santa / Mountain Balm

Insect Bites and Stings
Borage
Broom Snakeweed
Buffaloberry
Coltsfoot
Goldenrod
Goldenseal*
Lemon Balm
Mesquite
Saltbush
Red Clover*
Seneca Snakeroot*
Tobacco*
Witch Hazel

Insect Repellents and Insecticides
Goldenseal*
Mint
Osha
Rabbit Tobacco
Sweetgrass
Yarrow*

Insomnia
Chamomile
Hops
(Desert) Lavender
Lemon Balm
Oats
Passionflower*
Rabbit Tobacco
Skullcap*
Valerian
Wild Lettuce

Intestinal Worms
Gentiana
Garlic / Wild Garlic
Goldenseal*
Oregon Grape
Wormwood*

Irritable Bowel Syndrome
Valerian

Itching
Feverwort
Mint
Yellow Dock*

J

Jaundice
Boswellia*
Horsetail
Rosemary*

Joint Pain and Other Joint Problems
Cattail
Cedar*
Chickweed*
Damiana*
Devil's Claw*
Feverwort
Gentiana
Hawthorn
Nettle
Oak
(White) Pine
Rosemary*
Yellow Dock*
Yerba Santa / Mountain Balm
Yucca

K

Kidney Function and Problems, Including Kidney Stones
Borage
Dandelion
Flaxseed
Goldenrod
Horsetail
Juniper*
Oak
Saw Palmetto
Skullcap*
Stoneseed
Uva Ursi*
Wild Carrot*
Wild Lettuce
Wild Rose

L

Labor – see **Childbirth**

Laryngitis
Goldenrod
(White) Pine
Poke Root
Wild Black Cherry

Laxative – see **Constipation**

Libido
Damiana*
Saw Palmetto (for men)
Sarsaparilla* (for men)

Lice Treatment
California Poppy*

Liver Problems, Disease, and Health
Angelica*
Cleavers
Dandelion
(Desert) Lavender
Sarsaparilla*

Low Energy - see **Energy**

Lyme Disease
Cat's Claw*

M

Malaria
Boneset
Dogwood
Gentiana

Mastitis (lactational)
Poke Root

Measles
Dogwood
Sassafras

Memory
(American) Ginseng*
Rosemary*

Menopausal Symptoms
Black Cohosh*
Chasteberry*
Evening Primrose
Flaxseed
Red Clover*
Sage
St. John's Wort
Wild Yam*

Menorrhagia – see **Bleeding**

Menstrual Cramps and Pain
Angelica*
Black Cohosh*
Black Haw
Blue Cohosh*
Chamomile
Damiana*
Evening Primrose
Lemon Balm
Skullcap*
Wild Yam*

Menstrual Problems and Irregularities
Blue Cohosh*
Damiana*
Skullcap*
Uva Ursi*
Wild Carrot*

Migraines
(American) Feverfew
Feverfew*

Morning Sickness
Mint
Ginger

Motion Sickness
Mint
Ginger

Mouth Ulcers and Other Problems – see **Gum and Mouth Problems**

Mumps Symptoms
Elderflower (berries)

Poke Root

Muscle Problems – Aches, Cramps, Fatigue, and Spasms
Angelica*
Arnica*
Boneset
California Poppy*
Centaury
Chamomile
Comfrey
Dandelion
Devil's Claw*
Evening Primrose
Gentiana
(American) Ginseng*
Mint
Mullein
Passionflower*
Rosemary*
Sage
Saltbush
Valerian
White Willow*
Wild Yam*
Witch Hazel

N

Nausea
Chamomile
Feverwort
Horsemint*
Mint

Nervous Conditions
Chamomile
Damiana*
Oats
Skullcap*
Wild Black Cherry
Wild Lettuce

Neuralgia
Chamomile
Poke Root
Rosemary*
Skullcap*
St.John's Wort

Night Sweats
Black Cohosh*
Red Clover*
Sage

Nosebleeds (regular)
Horsetail
(Desert) Lavender
Oregon Grape
Yarrow*

Osteoarthritis
Devil's Claw*
Yucca

Pain
Arnica*
Black Cohosh*
Boneset
California Poppy*
Comfrey
Echinacea
(American) Ginseng*
Juniper*
Poke Root
Rosemary*
Skullcap*
Tobacco*
White Willow*
Wild Yam*
Yucca

Pancreas Troubles
Cat's Claw*
Uva Ursi*

Parkinson's Disease Symptoms
Elderflower (berries)
Garlic / Wild Garlic
Red Clover*

Pleurisy
Angelica*
Feverwort

PMS
Angelica*
Black Cohosh*
Chasteberry*
Skullcap*

Pneumonia
Dogwood
Honeysuckle
Mint
Nettle
(White) Pine
Rabbit Tobacco
Thyme
Wild Black Cherry

Poison Antidote
Tobacco*

Prostate Conditions
Horsetail
Prickly Pear Cactus
Saw Palmetto

Psoriasis
Burdock*
Red Clover*
Sarsaparilla*
St. John's Wort
Witch Hazel

Purgative
Poke Root

R

Rashes – see **Skin Disorders**

Reproductive System
Blue Cohosh*
Skullcap*

Respiratory Problems
Broom Snakeweed
Cedar*
Echinacea
Elderflower
Evening Primrose
Garlic / Wild Garlic
Honeysuckle
Horsemint*
Mint
Mullein
Osha
Plantain
Red Clover*
Thyme
Yarrow*
Yellow Dock*

Restlessness Including Restless Legs Syndrome and Restless Sleep
Chamomile
Hops
Skullcap*
Valerian
Wild Lettuce
Yerba Santa / Mountain Balm

Rheumatism and Rheumatoid Arthritis
Arnica*
Black Cohosh*
Black Haw
Blue Cohosh*
Boneset
Boswellia*
Cat's Claw*
Chamomile
Chickweed*
Devil's Claw*
Garlic / Wild Garlic
Hemlock (native)
Horsemint*
Horsetail
Juniper*
Nettle
Poke Root
Sarsaparilla*
Slippery Elm*
Stoneseed
White Willow*
Wild Yam*
Yew

Ringworm
Aloe Vera
Garlic / Wild Garlic
Milkweed
Oak
Sarsaparilla*
Yellow Dock*

S

Sciatica
Black Cohosh*
St. John's Wort

Scarlet Fever
Wild Ginger

Scurvy
Hemlock (native)
Wild Rose

Sedative / Sleep Aid
Black Haw
California Poppy*
Damiana*
Hops
Skullcap*
Stoneseed
Valerian
Wild Black Cherry
Wild Lettuce

Shingles
Echinacea
St. John's Wort

Sinus Problems
Angelica*
Elderflower
Goldenrod
Goldenseal*
Osha
Rabbit Tobacco

Skin Disorders, Conditions, Irritations, and Health
Borage
Burdock*
Cedar*
Chickweed*
Devil's Claw*
Dogwood
Elderflower
Evening Primrose
Feverwort
(American) Ginseng*
(Desert) Lavender
Mint
Pinon / Pinyon Pine
Prickly Pear Cactus
Rabbit Tobacco
Red Clover*
Rosemary*
Saltbush
Sarsaparilla*
Slippery Elm*
Sweetgrass
Thyme
Tobacco*
Uva Ursi*
Western Skunk Cabbage
Wild Carrot*
Witch Hazel
Yellow Dock*

Snakebites
Broom Snakeweed
Gentiana
Goldenseal*
Plantain
Seneca Snakeroot*
Tobacco*
Wild Carrot*

Sores
Broom Snakeweed
Buckbrush
Burdock*
Devil's Claw*
Echinacea
(American) Ginseng*
Goldenseal*
Hemlock (native)
Horsemint*
Pinon / Pinyon Pine
(White) Pine
Rabbit Tobacco
Saltbush
Western Skunk Cabbage
Witch Hazel
Yellow Dock*

Sore Eyes – see **Eye Problems**

Sore Throat and Throat Ulcers – see **Throat Conditions**

Spider Bites
Saltbush
Slippery Elm*

Sprains
Arnica*
Cattail
Comfrey
Oak
Poke Root
Yerba Santa / Mountain Balm
Yucca

Stings – see **Insect Bites**

Stomach Problems
Blackberry
Cattail

Dandelion
Goldenseal*
Hawthorn
Juniper*
Milkweed
Mint
Slippery Elm*
Wild Black Cherry
Wormwood*
Yellow Dock*

Stomach Ulcers
Aloe Vera
Garlic / Wild Garlic
Goldenseal*

Stress / Tension
Damiana*
Hops
Lemon Balm
Skullcap*
Valerian
Wild Lettuce

Sunscreen
Hemlock (Eastern)

Sunburn (to treat)
Aloe Vera
Hemlock (Eastern)
St. John's Wort
Witch Hazel

Sweating (to promote)
- see **Diaphoretic**

Sweating (excessive)
Black Cohosh*
Lemon Balm
Sage

Swelling - see **Inflammation**

T

Tinnitus
Black Cohosh*
Mullein

Throat Conditions – Ulcers, Sore Throats, Tonsillitis
Blackberry
Borage
Buckbrush
California Poppy*
Chamomile
Chickweed*
Coltsfoot
Dandelion
Echinacea
Elderflower (berries)
Flaxseed
Goldenrod
Goldenseal*
Hemlock (native)
Honeysuckle
Mesquite
Oak
Osha
Poke Root
Sage
Skullcap*
Slippery Elm*
Sumac
Thyme
Western Skunk Cabbage
Wild Black Cherry
Wild Rose

Toothache
Blackberry
Chamomile
Dandelion
Hops
Plantain
Slippery Elm*
White Willow*
Yarrow*

Tonic
Dandelion
Nettle

Toxins (to eliminate)
Dandelion

Thyroid Function
Boswellia*

U

Ulcers (external)
Burdock*
Coltsfoot
(American) Ginseng*
Hemlock (native)
Slippery Elm*

Urinary Problems
Cleavers
Goldenrod
Horsemint*
Horsetail
Juniper*
Prickly Pear Cactus
Saw Palmetto
Stoneseed
Uva Ursi*
Wild Carrot*
Wild Rose

V

Vaginal Problems Including Dryness
Arnica*
Black Cohosh*
Flaxseed

Varicose Veins
St. John's Wort
Witch Hazel

Vertigo / Dizziness
Broom Snakeweed
Wild Ginger

W

Warts
Cedar*
Dandelion
Milkweed

Weight (to reduce)
Boswellia*
Wild Ginger

Whooping Cough
Blackberry
Broom Snakeweed
Coltsfoot
Goldenseal*
(White) Pine
Red Clover*
Wild Black Cherry
Wild Lettuce

Withdrawal Symptoms
Skullcap*

Worms – see **Intestinal Worms**

Wound Healing
Aloe Vera
Broom Snakeweed
Buffaloberry
Cattail
Cedar*
Chokeberry
Coltsfoot
Comfrey
Dogwood
Echinacea
Evening Primrose
Gentiana
Goldenrod
Goldenseal*
Hemlock (native)
Horsemint*
Horsetail
Juniper*
Mesquite
Milkweed
Mullein
Nettle
Osha
Passionflower*
Pinon / Pinyon Pine
(White) Pine
Prickly Pear Cactus
Saltbush
Seneca Snakeroot*
Thyme
Uva Ursi*
Western Skunk Cabbage
Wild Ginger
Yucca

Y

Yeast Infection
Uva Ursi*

Z

Zoster – see **Shingles**

The remedies listed in this dispensatory are the herbs of choice for Jacob; he acknowledges that there are many others available, but he can only attest to those that are in his personal herbal toolbox. By no means exhaustive, these are the herbs he has found most useful for the listed ailments.

Not sure how to use the herbs? Look now to PART 7, where your instructions await!

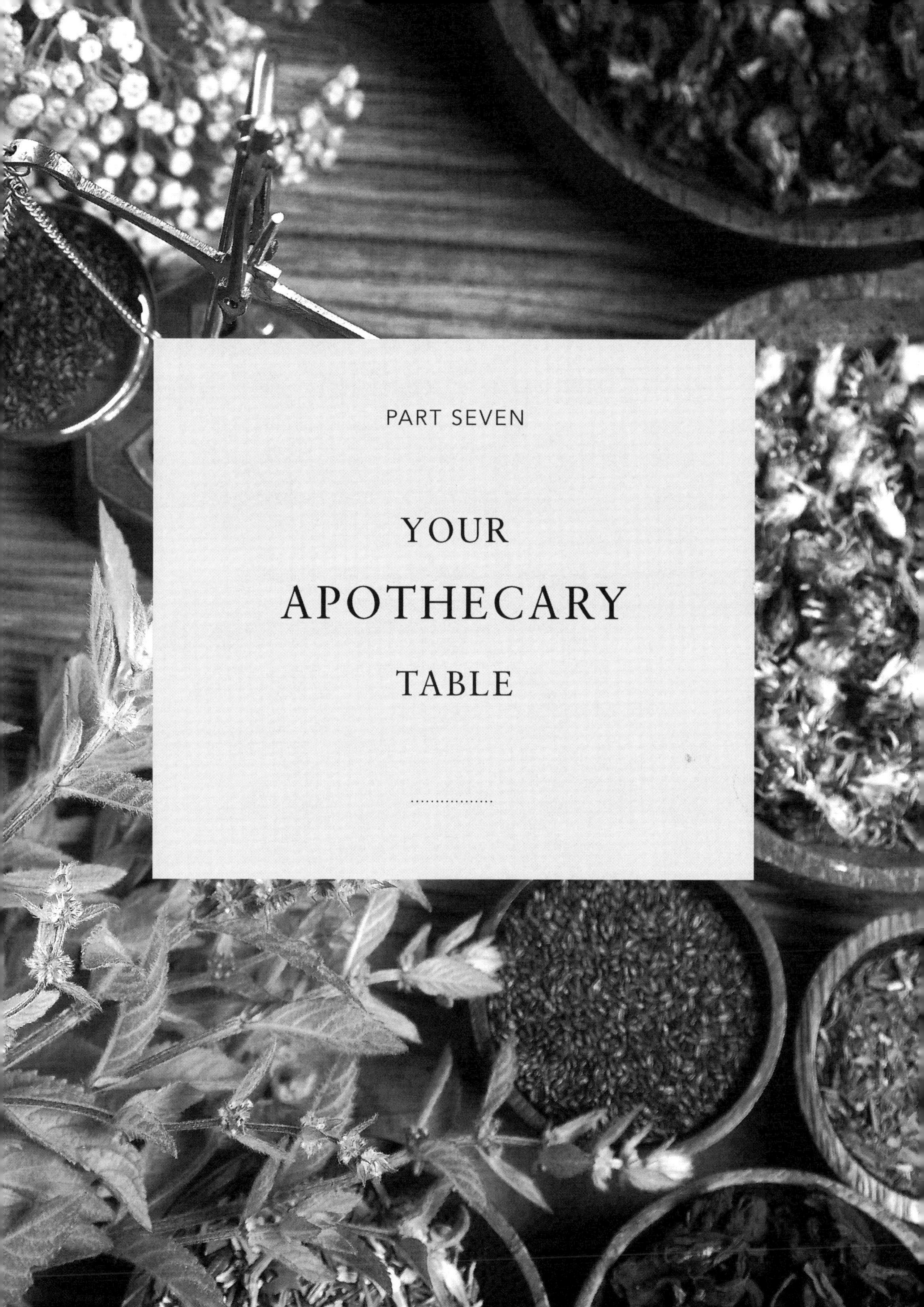

PART SEVEN

YOUR APOTHECARY TABLE

How to prepare and store your herbs for usage

How to make Compresses, Decoctions, Infusions, Ointments, Oils, Poultices, Syrups, and Tinctures

Herbs and plants in this book are not always available. Still, they can be preserved and stored in several ways, including drying parts of the plant, making infusions, tinctures, and syrups to take orally, ointments for topical use, and herb oils for use in cooking or healing balms. Suggestions for which herb is most suitable for each method are in PART 5 of this book.

A compress is applied directly to a wound or affected area. You can apply leaves, flowers, bark, roots, and herb oil. Compresses use an infusion of water, which is applied to the site using a flannel cloth. Cold compresses provide pain relief and often reduce swelling. Hot compresses ease arthritic or rheumatic pain combined with a hot water bottle or hot blanket.

A decoction is a technique used to extract ingredients in hot water when they are more challenging to access than flowers, e.g., bark, roots, and seeds. Plant pieces are cleaned and simmered over low heat to extract the ingredients without boiling. Then they are strained into containers, sealed, and stored. However, making a decoction when needed may be necessary, as they usually only last about 3-5 days.

An infusion involves immersing fresh or dried leaves, flowers, and sometimes soft fruit in boiling water to make a tea with herbal benefits. Always strain the tea before drinking.

An ointment is used on cuts and wounds topically on the skin. Jacob recommends using beeswax to mix the active oil or tincture into a creamy consistency, which you can apply easily. You can also use a little oil or tincture on a cotton swab applied directly to the area.

A (plant or herb) oil is made by infusing the oil with parts of the plant, e.g., leaves, stems, bark, and roots can all be used. Hot oil infusions and cold oil infusions depend on the ingredient wanted and whether it is destroyed by heat.

A poultice is from fresh or dried leaves, cones, flowers, or roots and is affixed to a wound, sting, or bruise with gauze.

A syrup is usually a sweetened liquid with active plant ingredients mixed with sugar as a preservative.

A tincture is an extraction of active ingredients using alcohol to create a very dense concentration. Alcohol will preserve the elements well for longer than is ordinarily possible. Tinctures are used when it is challenging to extract ingredients in water. Many substances can be destroyed by heat used in boiling techniques, so making a tincture is ideal for preserving the goodness of the herb in a form that you can store. Take a tincture orally using a dropper to place the liquid under the tongue or drop it into a glass of water and swallow.

1. How to Make a Compress

Native Americans used plant roots, such as cattails, by cutting the root in half and applying the substance directly to a clean wound. A compress often uses leaves, flowers, roots, bark, or herb oil made from these and is applied directly on wounds, bruises, stings, toothaches, or to the head for a headache. Cold compresses are used to provide pain relief and typically to reduce swelling. Hot compresses ease arthritic or rheumatic pain combined with a hot water bottle or hot blanket.

Herbs suitable for this method include:

Cattail roots are cut open, wrapped around a wound, and secured with raffia, string, or medical tape. Native Americans used cattails as emergency first aid since the root had antiseptic qualities.

Mullein and plantain leaves have antiseptic ingredients, so you can wrap them to clean wounds.

Aloe vera gel is taken from the interior of a spiked leaf, used directly on a wound, and covered with gauze.

2. How to Make a Decoction

You will need your chosen plant, a pot with some water to boil, and a sieve to strain your decoction into a sealed container.

Preparation Instructions:

A. Prepare a pot full of cold water. The quantity depends on the number of herbs you have. Use 1 teaspoon (5 g) of plant material per cup of water.

B. Bring the water and herbs to a boil but remember that boiling can reduce the active ingredients. So, watch it carefully and reduce the heat as soon as it boils.

C. Allow to steep for 20 minutes, strain the herbs through a sieve, and discard these into your compost bin.

D. Pour the resulting liquid into a sealed container and allow it to cool.

If you are mixing two separate decoctions, pour one of them and allow it to settle before adding the second. Label carefully and store in the refrigerator for about three days or so.

Herbs suitable for this method include:

Cat's Claw - use green or dried pods.

Hawthorn

Oak - use the inner bark to make a decoction. For sore throats, add drops to water for a gargle.

Goldenrod - the Chippewa used a root decoction internally and externally for cramps and as a decoction of dried leaves for fevers.

Stoneseed - use fresh or dried root.

3. How to Make an Infusion

You will need to add a teaspoon (5 g) of fresh or dried flowers, dried berries, roots, or leaves to boiling water. Strain the herbal or plant material and discard it before you drink the infusion. Adding the plant material to your compost pile is a way to give back to the land.

Herbs suitable for this method include:

Chamomile flowers - you can dry them, grind them into a powder, then infuse them.

Chickweed - the Cherokee dried the whole herb and made infusions with water utilizing it as a soothing cough mixture and for sore, hoarse throats. In addition, this infusion was used as an eyewash for infected eyes.

Cleavers tea - drinking this tea protects the bladder, the kidneys, and the liver.

Elderflowers - for sore eyes and conjunctivitis. Make an infusion of petals as an eyewash to rinse sore eyes. You can also drink some elderflower tea to relax.

Hawthorn - use fresh new growth.

Juniper berries - are especially recommended in tea for colic and flatulence. However, pregnant women are strongly advised to avoid them.

Nettle tea - is made from dried or fresh leaves.

Peppermint - infuse the leaves to reduce the body temperature and cool your body during heat waves.

Sage - leaves infused in water.

Rose - use the flower petals as an infusion for sore throats.

Rosehip - typically grated into a tea for very high levels of vitamin C. You may need to double strain to avoid the rosehip's sticky hairs.

Valerian - use dried roots for relaxation and to reduce stress.

4. How to Make an Ointment

Ointments do not contain water but usually use fats and oils with plant ingredients added. For example, you can use paraffin wax or petroleum jelly, but you can also use sunflower oil or almond oil with beeswax. Use 1 oz (28 g) of beeswax for 4 oz (118 ml) of vegetable oil. If you need a large amount, you can double up quantities, but it has a limited shelf life; use within three months. Ensure you label your container carefully with its contents and date of creation.

Preparation Instructions:

A. Place a bowl in a saucepan of hot water to melt the beeswax and simmer on low heat. When completely melted, remove the bowl carefully.

B. Now add an oil of your choice. Stir this and pour it into a sealed container. Recycled cosmetic jars work well.

C. When you apply the ointment, you can add powdered herbs; dried elderflower or mullein powder are both excellent plants to use.

Herbs suitable for this method include:

Chickweed - for skin infections and wounds, use the leaves to make a poultice or dry the leaves and use the powder as a wound healer. Shake it over the affected area and then use leaves as a poultice. You can add the powder to your ointment base and use it topically.

Cat's Claw - for sores, muscle pain, and arthritis.

Elderflowers - for sore eyes and conjunctivitis. Apply ointment around the eyes but not in the eyes. You can also make an infusion of petals as an eyewash to rinse sore eyes.

Hops - use the brown female cones picked in the fall.

Mullein - you can make leaves into an ointment.

Aloe Vera - the gel is a natural ointment that promotes healing. Add it to your ointment base and apply it directly to any wound.

5. How to Make a Plant or Herb Oil

First, decide which oil is suitable for your use. For instance, olive oil is good for strong-tasting herbs, and sunflower oil has a lighter taste and is more suitable for delicate flavors like tarragon. Almond oil tastes slightly sweeter. Hot oils infused with herbs or plants will last several months. Ensure you label your container carefully with its contents and date of creation.

Some volatile compounds tend to escape in hot oil infusions, so Jacob recommends cold oil infusions, as they retain their medicinal qualities better.

You will need:

A container with a lid to mix the oil and herbs
A muslin bag and a jug to strain the infused oil
Your chosen herb (see quantities of the fresh or dried herb under "B" below)
Have a supply of clean, sterilized containers to store the oil

Preparation Instructions:

A. Fill the container with herb or plant parts.

B. Top up the container with the selected oil, covering the fresh herbs with an extra inch of oil at the top. You can fill the container with half herbs and half oil if dried herbs are used. Finally, seal the container with the lid.

C. Place the container on a sunny windowsill. If this isn't possible, cover your container with a towel or paper bag somewhere warm to help infusion.

D. Turn the jar daily and shake it gently.

E. After letting it infuse for two weeks, strain the mixture through a muslin bag into a jug.

F. Squeeze the bag to extract all the infused oil. Discard the herbs or plants into your compost pile for your garden.

G. Repeat these steps with new flowers or herbs using the same oil, and your mixture will double in strength.

H. Finally, store your oil in sealed, sterilized jars in a cupboard away from direct sunlight.

Herbs suitable for this method include:

Comfrey - flowers and leaves.

Juniper - collect berries in the fall and use these crushed in oil to make an ointment for topical use on the skin to treat rheumatic pain. Not for pregnant women.

Lavender - collect flowers in bloom, soak them in oil, strain, and resoak with new flower heads; strain again. Do this three times, then do a final oil strain and store it in a dark space.

Marigold petals.

Mullein - collect flowers as they open and add them to the oil. Allow them to soak in the oil.

St. John's Wort - collect flowers and use them fresh or dried.

6. How to Make a Poultice

A poultice is typically made from fresh or dried leaves or roots and fixed with gauze to a wound, sting, or bruise. If you use fresh leaves, they will stick to the injury or area more easily if you apply a little oil first.
If using flowers or *leaves:* Pick fresh leaves if possible. You can chop large leaves like comfrey or mullein, and they are easier to wrap around limbs when large. Heat the leaves in a bit of water to warm them, squeeze out excess liquid, and apply the leaves to the sore area.

If using bark: Collect small amounts and check if it should be used fresh or dried. Then, place a portion of the plant material on the affected area, cover it with gauze, and leave it on for at least three hours. Replace with new leaves when you remove the poultice.

Herbs suitable for this method include:

Borage (a poultice of crushed borage leaves will relieve stings)
Chickweed
Comfrey
(American) Ginseng
Hawthorn bark
Hops
Mullein
Plantain

7. How to Make a Syrup

Rosehip syrup is the traditional method used worldwide for sore throats and colds and as a general tonic for winter blues. Rosehips contain twenty times the amount of vitamin C as oranges! You can also conserve it for winter use by storing it in sealed containers in a cool, dark place or the refrigerator. Ensure your container is carefully labeled with its contents and date of creation.

You will need:

4 cups (0.95 l) thoroughly washed rosehips, elderberries, or similar
2 cups (0.47 l) of water
1 cup (227 g) of sugar
A saucepan with a lid
A muslin bag
A sterilized container with a lid

Preparation Instructions:

A. Boil the rosehips or berries for 20 minutes in a covered saucepan.

B. Once boiled, strain the fruit through the muslin and return the clear juice to the saucepan.

C. Add the sugar to the strained juice, stir well, and boil for five minutes. Ensure that the sugar has completely dissolved and the syrup has thickened.

D. Keep in a cool, dark place in a sterilized, airtight container or refrigerate until ready for use.

Herbs suitable for this method include:

Rosehips - pick after the first frosts. They should be bright red.

Elderflower - use the black, ripe berries. Discard the stem.

8. How to Make a Tincture

Herbs contain many active ingredients which work in various ways for different ailments. However, it is difficult to extract them in water. In addition, many substances can be destroyed by heat used in boiling techniques, so making a tincture is ideal for preserving the goodness of the herb in a form you can store.

A tincture is a method of saving the extract of an herb using alcohol and water, which provides a very dense concentration. Tinctures sold commercially usually use ethyl alcohol as a base. However, vodka or brandy is suitable for homemade mixtures, as these will preserve the herb mixture for approximately two years. Ensure you label your container carefully with its contents and date of creation.

You will need:

A large container with a lid, preferably glass, to place the liquid and herbs in

A muslin bag to place the herbs in to soak in the chosen alcohol preservative
Your chosen herb (see quantities of fresh or dried herb below)

Preparation Instructions:

A. Pour the alcohol and water into the container. The mix is 25% alcohol to 75% water.

B. Next, fill a muslin bag with your chosen herb and place this in the container. Securely tie the bag at the top so the herb does not escape but sits in the liquid to infuse it. For fresh herbs, use an equal amount of plant-to-alcohol ratio. For dried herbs, use a one to four plant-to-alcohol ratio.

C. Shake the container gently every day to encourage the herb to infuse fully.

D. After two weeks (or even up to six weeks), remove the muslin bag and squeeze it into the mixture.

E. Decant the tincture to sterilized bottles. These bottles should be dark so that natural light will not contaminate the strength or the color. Then store it in a cupboard away from natural sunlight.

Can't take alcohol?

You can substitute apple cider vinegar in tinctures for children or anyone for whom alcohol intake is not recommended. These can also be used as delicious salad dressings. However, due to the lower preservative nature of the vinegar compared to alcohol, this method is recommended for use with dried herbs only. Also, please note vinegar tinctures have a relatively shorter shelf life, around twelve months.

How to Dry Plants

See suggestions under the plant name (PARTS 4 and 5) for the best times to pick flowers, twigs, bark, and roots.

Flowers like lavender can be dried by picking some flowering stems and hanging them up in a dry place, out of direct sunshine.

Seeds like flaxseed or evening primrose can be arranged on clean paper and left to dry. After 4-5 days, store them in a dark glass jar and process as required.

Cut twigs with a sharp pair of scissors or pruning shears and dry upside down.

The bark should be harvested in small quantities to avoid damaging the tree.

Roots are challenging to harvest and may damage the health of the plant. Check the correct time to pick, dry, and make decoctions, oils, infusions, or tinctures.

Herbs should be kept on the stem, shaken to remove soil and bugs, and washed only very lightly. Lay out on clean paper or cloth. Once no noticeable moisture is apparent, remove any dead, moldy, or lower leaves and tie small bundles together. Place upside down in labeled paper bags with small holes punched in them to allow the drying process to continue. Place somewhere warm and airy. After two weeks, depending on the herb, you can crumble the leaves into food or grind them into powder when needed for remedies. Herbs with a higher moisture content may take longer than others to dry out. After that, you can store them in an airtight, labeled container. Never use moldy herbs, and discard all of them after a year.

Jacob asks that if you need to purchase rather than collect herbs, please buy only organic products that have both honored the land and will serve you best in the healing process.

CONCLUSION

Conclusion

"...everything on the earth has a purpose, every disease an herb to cure it, and every person a mission. This is the Indian theory of existence."

MOURNING DOVE, SALISH, 1888-1936

We end as we began with an acknowledgment of the bounty our planet provides and also an understanding that Mother Nature can help to heal us using plant knowledge while we take the time to care for our natural world. Jacob has detailed 101 herbs that he believes are the most valuable and effective in this book. You have learned about different herbs and plants that his ancestors used and how they can now provide natural homemade remedies, teas, and tinctures for any aches and pains you feel.

From the beginning of this book, he has encouraged you to look carefully at your whole environment as a healing source and work alongside Mother Nature in searching for natural remedies. By now, you know the value of plants to aid your relaxation, rectify any imbalances in energy, and assist you and your family in avoiding over-the-counter medication. In addition, you are confident that herbal medicines have fewer side effects than conventional medicine. You should be aware of the plants that grow locally in your area, and perhaps you have started cultivating some yourself. Maybe you have treated a sore throat with elderberry or rosehip syrup to chase away a cold or flu!

Next Steps for Readers

"I picture each and every one of my readers with a sacred space for your herbs and ceremonies, your medicine bag, and this guidebook. My wish for you is that your apothecary shelves are packed with jars, tinctures, and the right dried herbs for the winter blues or to banish any everyday health problem you and your family may face. I hope that having an honest relationship with the meadows, forests, or mountains where you collect has brought more peace and calm into your life. Also, now, herb collection is an activity you enjoy regularly. Maybe you have joined forces with friends locally with similar intentions, and there are groups of protectors of nature around the country, all tending to their patch with love and care".

"All who have enjoyed reading this book are actively working alongside the Cherokee tribe (and other Native American Nations in the US). Together, we are working hand in hand with the natural world, seeking to bring harmony, and understanding that our lives and ailments are part of a spiritual, holistic way of life that can provide the healing we need."

A Request and a Blessing

If this book has helped you on your path to a healthier life, then Jacob would be very grateful if you could review it on Amazon and describe to new readers why it has been helpful for you. This way, the "good" energy continues, and his book can sit proudly on other bookshelves where healing and relaxation are needed.

"Before we departed on any collecting trip, my grandmother used to bless the home we were leaving and the road we chose to travel, asking the Creator to accompany us. Use this blessing daily, asking for the wind and weather to be kind to you in your plant collection work and life. Ask for a rainbow to go along with you to aid your journey and safely escort you back home."

Jacob Black

"Medicine Wheel & the Four Directions"

May the Warm Winds of Heaven
Blow softly upon your house.
May the Great Spirit
Bless all who enter there.
May your Moccasins
Make happy tracks
In many snows,
And may the Rainbow
Always touch your shoulder.

CHEROKEE PRAYER BLESSING

References and Index of Herbs

Part 1

https://unitedplantsavers.org/the-original-medicinal-plant-gatherers-conservationists/

Part 2

Christopher Rybak and Amanda Decker-Fitts, 2009, Understanding Native American Healing Practices.
CCPQ_A_427264_P 333..342 (enmu.edu)
https://en.wikipedia.org/wiki/The_red_road
http://www.mythencyclopedia.com/Wa-Z/Woman-Who-Fell-From-the-Sky.html
https://thewildwest.org/lakotaindiansuseofthesweatlodge/
https://www.legendsofamerica.com/na-medicinebag/
Plant Details :: Storytelling (csusm.edu)
https://www.northerncollege.ca/northern-college-breaks-ground-on-sacred-garden-at-timmins-campus/
D Bigfoot and M.C. Dunlap, 2006, Storytelling as a Healing Tool for American Indians.
https://theherbalacademy.com/the-herbal-healing-practices-of-native-americans/
http://www.inquiriesjournal.com/articles/1849/the-role-of-native-american-healing-traditions-within-allopathic-medicine

Part 3

Plant Details :: Medicinal Plants (csusm.edu)
https://www.irishtimes.com/news/health/why-are-doctors-so-against-alternative-medicine-1.188177
https://www.ecowatch.com/herbal-medicine-2009451657.html
https://www.theguardian.com/society/2018/aug/30/modern-medicine-major-threat-public-health
https://www.open.edu/openlearn/body-mind/health/health-sciences/herbal-medicine

Part 4

see index of herbs and
https://www.special-dictionary.com/proverbs/source/n/native_american_arapaho_proverb/92576.htm

Part 5

see index of herbs and
Herbs to Avoid During Pregnancy (utep.edu)
https://www.legendsofamerica.com/na-herbs/
https://www.herbalgram.org/resources/commission-e-monographs/
https://www.usp.org/
https://www.pharmacopoeia.com/
https://www.ahpa.org/

Part 6

https://www.legendsofamerica.com/na-medicine/
Compiled by Kathy Weiser/Legends of America, updated February 2020.

Part 7

Plant Details :: Plant Drying Process (csusm.edu)
Plant Details :: Plant Making Medicines (csusm.edu)
https://traditionalcookingschool.com/health-and-nutrition/how-to-make-and-use-an-herbal-decoction/
Herbal tinctures: 6 types and recipes (medicalnewstoday.com)
DIY SHTF Healing Salve - Ask a Prepper

How to Dry and Store Fresh Garden Herbs (thespruce.com)
Traditional Alaskan Rose Hip Simple Syrup Recipe (thespruceeats.com)
https://www.healthbenefitstimes.com/american-dogwood/

Conclusion
https://www.legendsofamerica.com/na-medicine/
http://www.sapphyr.net/natam/quotes-nativeamerican.htm

1. Aloe Vera - page 67
https://www.wikihow.com/Use-Aloe-Vera-to-Treat-Rheumatoid-Arthritis
Oral administration of Aloe vera gel, anti-microbial and anti-inflammatory herbal remedy, stimulates cell-mediated immunity and antibody production in a mouse model – PMC (nih.gov)
9 Herbs to Fight Arthritis Pain: Aloe Vera, Ginger, and More (healthline.com)
Plant Details :: Aloe Vera(ERO) (csusm.edu)
Plant Details :: Zavila (csusm.edu)
https://www.medicalnewstoday.com/articles/320911#home-remedies
https://www.healthline.com/nutrition/stomach-ulcer-remedies#

2. Angelica - page 68
How to Harvest and Use Angelica | Gardener's Path (gardenerspath.com)
https://www.rxlist.com/angelica/supplements.htm
https://chiavaye.com/blogs/endometriosis/herbs-for-vaginal-dryness
https://gobotany.nativeplanttrust.org/species/angelica/atropurpurea/#

3. Arnica - page 69
Herbs, Plants, and Healing Properties – Legends of America
Plant Details :: Arnica (Edited by Diaz) (csusm.edu)
https://www.fs.usda.gov/detail/boise/learning/nature-science/?cid=fsed_009691#:~:text=Externally%2C%20arnica

4. Blackberry - page 35
23 Medicinal Plants the Native Americans Used on a Daily Basis (map-expo.com)
Herbs, Plants, and Healing Properties – Page 2 – Legends of America
https://urbansurvivalsite.com/native-american-herbs-recipes/
https://www.gardeningknowhow.com/edible/fruits/blackberries/growing-blackberry-bushes.htm

5. Black Cohosh - page 70
https://www.organicfacts.net/black-cohosh-tea.html
Alternative Tinnitus Treatments | Arches Tinnitus Formula | Natural Treatment for Tinnitus
Herbs, Plants, and Healing Properties – Page 2 – Legends of America
https://www.motherlove.com/blogs/all/herbs-to-ease-labor-birth-and-recovery
https://chiavaye.com/blogs/endometriosis/herbs-for-vaginal-dryness
https://www.sciencedirect.com/science/article/abs/pii/S0378874112002127

6. Black Haw - page 70
https://wholisticmatters.com/herb-detail/cramp-bark/
https://www.healthline.com/nutrition/cramp-bark-guelder-rose
https://en.wikipedia.org/wiki/Viburnum_prunifolium#
https://www.indigo-herbs.co.uk/natural-health-guide/benefits/black-haw
Hamel, Paul B. and Mary U. Chiltoskey, 1975 – page 62
Herbs, Plants, and Healing Properties – Page 2 – Legends of America

7. Blue Cohosh - page 71
https://www.motherlove.com/blogs/all/herbs-to-ease-labor-birth-and-recovery
https://cornellbotanicgardens.org/plant/early-blue-cohosh/
https://wa.kaiserpermanente.org/kbase/topic.jhtml?docId=hn-2048000
https://www.webmd.com/vitamins/ai/ingredientmono-987/blue-cohosh#
Hamel, Paul B. and Mary U. Chiltoskey, 1975 – page 30

8. Boneset - page 72
Boneset Uses, Benefits & Side Effects – Drugs.com Herbal Database
Herbs, Plants, and Healing Properties – Page 2 – Legends of America
http://artsandsciences.sc.edu/appalachianenglish/node/344
https://www.herbalgram.org/resources/herbalgram/issues/125/table-of-contents/hg125-orgnews-ahpboneset/
https://thepracticalherbalist.com/herbal-memoirs/using-herbs-build-repair-bones/
Hamel, Paul B. and Mary U. Chiltoskey, 1975 – page 26

9. Borage - page 72
https://herbclass.com/borage/
https://www.facebook.com/BotanyClinic/posts/borage-flowerscientific-classificationkingdom-plantaeunranked-angiospe rmsborago-/907987806000397/
https://www.webmd.com/vitamins-and-supplements/what-to-know-about-borage
https://gobotany.nativeplanttrust.org/species/borago/officinalis/

10. Boswellia - page 73
9 Herbs to Fight Arthritis Pain: Aloe Vera, Ginger, and More (healthline.com)
Boswellia sacra essential oil induces tumor cell-specific apoptosis and suppresses tumor aggressiveness in cultured human breast cancer cells – PMC (nih.gov)
https://www.verywellhealth.com/the-health-benefits-of-boswellia-89549
Herbs, Plants, and Healing Properties – Page 2 – Legends of America
https://www.ncbi.nlm.nih.gov/pmc/articles/PMC3309643/
https://www.ncbi.nlm.nih.gov/pmc/articles/PMC3532773/
https://www.wonderlabs.com/blog/boswellia-can-assist-in-weight-loss#:~:text=Boswellia

11. Broom Snakeweed - page 74
https://plants.usda.gov/DocumentLibrary/plantguide/pdf/cs_gusa2.pdf
Herbs, Plants, and Healing Properties – Page 2 – Legends of America
https://www.nps.gov/para/learn/nature/snakeweed.htm#:~:text=Snakeweed
https://nativeamericanmuseum.blogspot.com/search?q=broom+snakeweed

12. Buckbrush - page 38
23 Medicinal Plants the Native Americans Used on a Daily Basis (map-expo.com)
Herbs, Plants, and Healing Properties – Page 2 – Legends of America
https://urbansurvivalsite.com/native-american-herbs-recipes/
https://www.cherokeephoenix.org/culture/buckbrush-a-cherokee-source-for-basketry/article_4ea553af-d581-5d32-b872-5a83aa9cf940.html
https://keys2liberty.wordpress.com/tag/buck-brush/

13. Buffaloberry - page 75
http://www.naturalmedicinalherbs.net/herbs/s/shepherdia-canadensis=buffalo-berry.php
https://pfaf.org/user/plant.aspx?latinname=Shepherdia+canadensis
https://aihd.ku.edu/foods/buffaloberry.html
Herbs, Plants, and Healing Properties – Page 2 – Legends of America

https://mpgnorth.com/field-guide/elaeagnaceae/canada-buffaloberry

14. Burdock - page 75
BURDOCK – NativeTech: Indigenous Plants & Native Uses in the Northeast
Herbs, Plants, and Healing Properties – Page 2 – Legends of America
https://www.webmd.com/diet/health-benefits-burdock-root#1
https://plantura.garden/uk/flowers-perennials/burdock/burdock-overview
https://www.gaiaherbs.com/blogs/seeds-of-knowledge/herbs-for-gallbladder
https://doctor.ndtv.com/living-healthy/5-herbs-which-can-help-in-dissolving-uric-acid-1903732
https://www.webmd.com/diet/health-benefits-burdock-root#1

15. California Poppy - page 76
Plant Details :: California poppy (csusm.edu)
https://www.sierraclub.org/ventana/santa-cruz/blog/2014/08/native-plant-week-california-poppy-escholtzia-californica
Plant Details :: Sedative (csusm.edu)
http://www.storey.com/article/8-native-plants-native-medicine/

16. Cat's Claw - page 77
Five Facts: Cat's-claw vine in Florida – Florida Museum Science (ufl.edu)
9 Herbs to Fight Arthritis Pain: Aloe Vera, Ginger, and More (healthline.com)
Cat's Claw | NCCIH (nih.gov)
https://www.indigo-herbs.co.uk/shop/buy/cats-claw-tincture-100ml
https://nurservicio.com/cats-claw/
Cat�s Claw – Uses (kaiserpermanente.org)
Cat�s Claw – Health Information Library | PeaceHealth
Cat's Claw: Benefits, Uses, Dosage, and Side Effects – EvidenceLive
Cat's claw: beans from the thorny desert tree. – (ethnoherbalist.com)
Plant Details :: Acacia (csusm.edu)
Herbs, Plants, and Healing Properties – Page 3 – Legends of America
https://lymeguide.info/cats-claw/#
https://www.ncbi.nlm.nih.gov/books/NBK548323/#:~:text=Cat's%20claw

17. Cattail - page 39
https://www.farmersalmanac.com/cooking-wild-edible-cattails-25374
23 Medicinal Plants the Native Americans Used on a Daily Basis (map-expo.com)
Plant Details :: Cat-tail (csusm.edu)
Herbs, Plants, and Healing Properties – Page 3 – Legends of America
https://urbansurvivalsite.com/native-american-herbs-recipes/
https://parade.com/844248/juliebawdendavis/grow-cattails-in-your-water-garden-and-pond/
https://jamesknellermd.com/11-medicinal-plants-used-to-cure-everything/#:~:text=Cattail

18. Cedar - page 78
The Legend of the Cedar Tree (rkdn.org)
http://www.native-languages.org/legends-cedar
Herbs, Plants, and Healing Properties – Page 3 – Legends of America
https://prairieedge.com/tribe-scribe/native-american-sacred-herb-flat-cedar/

19. Centaury - page 78
Centaury Uses, Benefits & Dosage – Drugs.com Herbal Database
http://medicinalherbinfo.org/000Herbs2016/1herbs/centaury/
https://wa.kaiserpermanente.org/kbase/topic.jhtml?docId=hn-3655009
https://earthnotes.tripod.com/centaury.htm

20. Chamomile - page 79
23 Medicinal Plants the Native Americans Used on a Daily Basis (map-expo.com)
https://www.plantgrower.org/chamomile.html
https://www.northeastsuperfoods.com/blog/2017/11/10/our-own-wild-chamomile
Plant Details :: Manzanilla (csusm.edu)
Herbs, Plants, and Healing Properties – Page 3 – Legends of America

21. Chasteberry - page 80
https://www.verywellhealth.com/what-is-chasteberry-2721967
https://www.healthline.com/nutrition/vitex
Herbs, Plants, and Healing Properties – Page 3 – Legends of America
https://pubmed.ncbi.nlm.nih.gov/18577418/

22. Chickweed - page 80
Chickweed: Benefits, Side Effects, Precautions, and Dosage (healthline.com)
Herbs, Plants, and Healing Properties – Page 3 – Legends of America
https://www.outdoorapothecary.com/chickweed-identification/#:~:text=Chickweed
https://nativeamericanmuseum.blogspot.com/2019/04/medicinal-monday-common-chickweed.html

23. Chokeberry - page 81
https://www.healthline.com/nutrition/aronia-berries
https://www.gardeningknowhow.com/ornamental/shrubs/aronia/aronia-harvest-time.htm
https://www.organicfacts.net/health-benefits/fruit/chokeberries.html
https://www.herbalgram.org/resources/herbalgram/issues/101/table-of-contents/hg101-herbpro-chokeberry/

24. Cleavers - page 82
https://www.verywellhealth.com/cleavers-health-benefits-5084341
https://www.indigo-herbs.co.uk/natural-health-guide/benefits/cleavers
https://www.traditionalmedicinals.com/articles/plants/cleavers-101/
https://www.healthygreensavvy.com/cleavers-plant-herb-benefits/

25. Coltsfoot - page 82
https://dsps.lib.uiowa.edu/roots/coltsfoot/
https://www.indigo-herbs.co.uk/natural-health-guide/benefits/coltsfoot
https://wildadirondacks.org/adirondack-wildflowers-coltsfoot-tussilago-farfara.html#:~
Coltsfoot | Tussilago farfara (wildadirondacks.org)
Herbs, Plants, and Healing Properties – Page 3 – Legends of America

26. Comfrey - page 83
Plant Details :: Consuelsa Mayor (csusm.edu)
Comfrey: ancient and modern uses – The Pharmaceutical Journal (pharmaceutical-journal.com)
https://eu.thenews-messenger.com/story/news/2021/04/07/master-gardener-comfrey-forgotten-herb/7103712002/#
https://www.ncbi.nlm.nih.gov/pmc/articles/PMC3491633/
Hamel, Paul B. and Mary U. Chiltoskey, 1975 – page 30

27. Damiana - page 83
https://www.live-native.com/damiana/
Herbs, Plants, and Healing Properties – Page 3 – Legends of America
https://www.peacehealth.org/medical-topics/id/hn-2077004#:~:text=Damiana
https://teapro.co.uk/damiana-ancient-aphrodisiac-love-potion/

28. Dandelion - page 41
Dandelion: Health Benefits, Uses, Side Effects, Dosage & Warnings (medicinenet.com)
Herbs, Plants, and Healing Properties – Page 3 – Legends of America
https://urbansurvivalsite.com/native-american-herbs-recipes/
https://homeguides.sfgate.com/grow-dandelions-indoors-pots-98287.html
https://www.gaiaherbs.com/blogs/seeds-of-knowledge/herbs-for-gallbladder
Hamel, Paul B. and Mary U. Chiltoskey, 1975 – page 31

29. Devil's Claw - page 84
23 Medicinal Plants the Native Americans Used on a Daily Basis (map-expo.com)
Devils claw plant for pain and osteoarthritis: does it work? (ethnoherbalist.com)
Herbs, Plants, and Healing Properties – Page 3 – Legends of America
https://doctor.ndtv.com/living-healthy/5-herbs-which-can-help-in-dissolving-uric-acid-1903732

30. Dogwood - page 85
https://www.missouribotanicalgarden.org/PlantFinder/PlantFinderDetails.aspx?kempercode=c280
https://www.healthbenefitstimes.com/american-dogwood/
Herbs, Plants, and Healing Properties – Page 3 – Legends of America
https://www.healthbenefitstimes.com/american-dogwood/
Hamel, Paul B. and Mary U. Chiltoskey, 1975 – page 32

31. Echinacea - page 86
Inflammation and Native American medicine: the role of botanicals | The American Journal of Clinical Nutrition | Oxford Academic (oup.com)
Echinacea for colds . . . is it effective? – (ethnoherbalist.com)
Herbs, Plants, and Healing Properties – Page 4 – Legends of America
https://www.mountsinai.org/health-library/herb/echinacea#
https://www.healthline.com/health/shingles-natural-treatment#6.-Homeopathic-or-herbal-remedies
https://efotg.sc.egov.usda.gov/references/public/va/NRCS_CulturallySignificantPlants_2010.pdf

32. Elderflower / berries - page 44
Native American Herbs May Slow Parkinson's Disease – Journal of Plant Medicines
3 benefits of black elderberry syrup for our immune system – (ethnoherbalist.com)
Plant Details :: Elderberry (csusm.edu)
Herbs, Plants, and Healing Properties – Page 4 – Legends of America
https://urbansurvivalsite.com/native-american-herbs-recipes/
https://theherbalacademy.com/10-elderflower-recipes-and-remedies/
https://blog.firsttunnels.co.uk/about-elderflower/
https://www.stlukes-stl.com/health-content/medicine/33/000112.htm
https://efotg.sc.egov.usda.gov/references/public/va/NRCS_CulturallySignificantPlants_2010.pdf
Hamel, Paul B. and Mary U. Chiltoskey, 1975 – page 33

33. Evening Primrose - page 86
Inflammation and Native American medicine: the role of botanicals | The American Journal of Clinical Nutrition | Oxford Academic (oup.com)
Herbs, Plants, and Healing Properties – Page 4 – Legends of America
https://www.nccih.nih.gov/health/evening-primrose-oil#:~:text=Native%20Americans
https://www.adkinsarboretum.org/programs_events/ipp/evening-primrose.html
Hamel, Paul B. and Mary U. Chiltoskey, 1975 – page 33

34. (American) Feverfew - page 87
American Feverfew | Missouri Department of Conservation (mo.gov)
https://www.uaex.uada.edu/yard-garden/resource-library/plant-week/american_feverfew-7-25-14.aspx#
https://www2.illinois.gov/dnr/education/CDIndex/AmericanFeverfew.pdf

35. Feverfew - page 88
How to Plant and Grow Feverfew | Gardener's Path (gardenerspath.com)
Feverfew (Tanacetum parthenium L.): A systematic review – PMC (nih.gov)
Herbs, Plants, and Healing Properties – Page 4 – Legends of America
https://nativeamericanmuseum.blogspot.com/2020/06/

36. Feverwort - page 88
https://pfaf.org/user/Plant.aspx?LatinName=Triosteum+perfoliatum
medicinal herbs: WILD COFFEE – Triosteum perfoliatum (naturalmedicinalherbs.net)
Herbs, Plants, and Healing Properties – Page 4 – Legends of America
https://www.wildflower.org/plants/result.php?id_plant=TRPE5
Hamel, Paul B. and Mary U. Chiltoskey, 1975 – page 39

37. Flaxseed - page 47
https://www.femina.in/wellness/home-remedies/banish-cough-with-these-foods-18051.html
Plant Details :: Linasa (csusm.edu)
https://urbansurvivalsite.com/native-american-herbs-recipes/
https://www.everydayhealth.com/diet/flaxseed-what-superfood-offers-how-add-it-your-diet/
https://www.gardeningknowhow.com/ornamental/flowers/flax/growing-flaxseed-plants.htm
https://chiavaye.com/blogs/endometriosis/herbs-for-vaginal-dryness
Hamel, Paul B. and Mary U. Chiltoskey, 1975 – page 34

38. Garlic / Wild Garlic - page 89
Native American Herbs May Slow Parkinson's Disease – Journal of Plant Medicines
Inflammation and Native American medicine: the role of botanicals | The American Journal of Clinical Nutrition | Oxford Academic (oup.com)
Herbs, Plants, and Healing Properties – Page 9 – Legends of America
https://www.stlukes-stl.com/health-content/medicine/33/000097.htm
https://www.medicalnewstoday.com/articles/320911#home-remedies
https://www.healthline.com/nutrition/stomach-ulcer-remedies#TOC_TITLE_HDR_11
https://efotg.sc.egov.usda.gov/references/public/va/NRCS_CulturallySignificantPlants_2010.pdf
https://pubmed.ncbi.nlm.nih.gov/11728237/#:~:text
Hamel, Paul B. and Mary U. Chiltoskey, 1975 – page 35

39. Gentiana - page 90
Herbs, Plants, and Healing Properties – Page 5 – Legends of America
https://www.rxlist.com/gentian/supplements.htm#:~:text=Gentiana
https://www.healthline.com/nutrition/gentian-root
https://www.indigo-herbs.co.uk/natural-health-guide/benefits/gentian

40. (American) Ginseng - page 90
Inflammation and Native American medicine: the role of botanicals | The American Journal of Clinical Nutrition | Oxford Academic (oup.com)
https://www.pregnancyfoodchecker.com/ginseng-safe-pregnancy-side-effects-benefits/
American Ginseng | nepollinatorweek (nebraskapollinatorweek.org)
https://www.mountsinai.org/health-library/herb/american-ginseng#

https://www.verywellhealth.com/american-ginseng-health-benefits-89218
https://pubmed.ncbi.nlm.nih.gov/29624410/#
https://www.nutraingredients.com/Article/2021/08/16/Ginseng-boosts-attention-and-memory-via-the-gut#
Hamel, Paul B. and Mary U. Chiltoskey, 1975 – page 36

41. Goldenrod - page 91
Herbs, Plants, and Healing Properties – Page 5 – Legends of America
https://www.herbalremediesadvice.org/goldenrod-plant.html#:~:text=Goldenrod
https://www.rxlist.com/goldenrod/supplements.htm#:~:text=Goldenrod
https://www.mountsinai.org/health-library/herb/goldenro
Hamel, Paul B. and Mary U. Chiltoskey, 1975 – page 36

42. Goldenseal - page 92
Inflammation and Native American medicine: the role of botanicals | The American Journal of Clinical Nutrition | Oxford Academic (oup.com)
Herbs, Plants, and Healing Properties – Page 5 – Legends of America
https://www.stlukes-stl.com/health-content/medicine/33/000097.htm
https://www.nccih.nih.gov/health/goldenseal#
https://draxe.com/nutrition/goldenseal/
https://www.healthline.com/health/goldenseal-cure-for-everything#
Hamel, Paul B. and Mary U. Chiltoskey, 1975 – page 36

43. Gravel Root / Joe Pye Weed - page 93
https://quod.lib.umich.edu/cgi/p/pod/dod-idx/joe-pye-joe-pyes-law-and-joe-pye-weed-the-history.pdf?c=mbot;idno=0497763.0056.303;format=pdf
https://www.motherearthliving.com/gardening/plant-profile/AN-HERB-TO-KNOW-Joe-Pye-Weed
https://www.outdoorapothecary.com/joe-pye-weed-uses/
http://medicinalherbinfo.org/000Herbs2016/1herbs/joe-pye-weed/
Hamel, Paul B. and Mary U. Chiltoskey, 1975 – pages 41/42

44. Hawthorn - page 93
Herbs, Plants, and Healing Properties – Page 5 – Legends of America
https://nativeamericanmuseum.blogspot.com/search?q=hawthorn
https://www.herbalgram.org/resources/herbalgram/issues/96/table-of-contents/herbalgram-96-herb-profile-hawthorn/
https://theherbalacademy.com/hawthorn-offerings/
Hamel, Paul B. and Mary U. Chiltoskey, 1975 – page 37

45. Hemlock - page 94
Herbs, Plants, and Healing Properties – Page 7 – Legends of America
https://jamanetwork.com/journals/jamadermatology/article-abstract/2471534#
https://www.arborday.org/programs/nationaltree/hemlock.cfm
https://thedruidsgarden.com/2014/01/02/sacred-tree-profile-eastern-hemlock-tsuga-canadensis-magic-mythology-and-qualities/
Hamel, Paul B. and Mary U. Chiltoskey, 1975 – page 38

46. Honeysuckle - page 95
23 Medicinal Plants the Native Americans Used on a Daily Basis (map-expo.com)
Herbs, Plants, and Healing Properties – Page 5 – Legends of America
https://www.rxlist.com/honeysuckle/supplements.htm
https://vnps.org/wildflower-year-2014-coral-honeysuckle-lonicera-sempervirens/

47. Hops - page 96
https://www.rxlist.com/hops/supplements.htm
https://www.encyclopedia.com/sports-and-everyday-life/food-and-drink/alcoholic-beverages/hops
Herbs, Plants, and Healing Properties – Page 5 – Legends of America
http://bioweb.uwlax.edu/bio203/s2009/sewalish_andr/Humulus%20Lupulus%20-%20Common%20Hops
Hamel, Paul B. and Mary U. Chiltoskey, 1975 – page 39

48. Horsemint - page 97
Herbs, Plants, and Healing Properties – Page 5 – Legends of America
http://www.nativenurseries.com/blog/horsemint#:~:text=Native%20Americans
http://www.naturalmedicinalherbs.net/herbs/m/monarda-punctata=horse-mint.php
http://medicinalherbinfo.org/000Herbs2016/1herbs/horsemint/
Hamel, Paul B. and Mary U. Chiltoskey, 1975 – page 39

49. Horsetail - page 97
https://extension.usu.edu/rangeplants/forbsherbaceous/horsetail
Horsetail: Health Benefits, Side Effects, Uses, Dose & Precautions (rxlist.com)
https://extension.usu.edu/rangeplants/forbsherbaceous/horsetail#
https://mcclungmuseum.utk.edu/2020/02/27/plant-of-the-month-rough-horsetail/
Hamel, Paul B. and Mary U. Chiltoskey, 1975 – page 39

50. Juniper - page 98
http://medicinalherbinfo.org/000Herbs2016/1herbs/juniper/
Juniper benefits: Native American use of the California juniper berry – (ethnoherbalist.com)
www.legendsofamerica.com/na-herbs/6/#J
https://www.rjwhelan.co.nz/conditions/prostate.html
https://www.wnyurology.com/content.aspx?chunkiid=21780

51. (Desert) Lavender - page 99
http://www.native-languages.org/legends-lavender.htm
Aromatherapy Article: DESERT LAVENDER (Hyptis emoryi) Essential Oil (phibeearomatics.com)
http://www.ethnoherbalist.com/southern-california-native-plants-medicinal/desert-lavender/
Sonoran Plant Profile: Desert Lavender – Desert Tortoise Botanicals (desertortoisebotanicals.com)
https://savorthesouthwest.blog/2014/07/25/desert-lavender/

52. Lemon Balm - page 100
https://www.moonmaidbotanicals.com/lemon-balm-uses.html
7 Important Herbal Remedies For Excessive Sweating – How To Get Rid Of Excessive Sweating | AyurvedicCure.com
Herbs, Plants, and Healing Properties – Page 6 – Legends of America
https://www.herbalgram.org/resources/expanded-commission-e/lemon-balm/
Hamel, Paul B. and Mary U. Chiltoskey, 1975 – page 24

53. Mesquite - page 101
https://foodtank.com/news/2014/04/mesquite-ancient-flour-of-the-future/#
https://www.nps.gov/articles/000/ethnobotany-of-mesquite-trees.htm
https://www.archaeologysouthwest.org/2020/06/12/a-brief-cultural-history-of-mesquite/
https://www.henriettes-herb.com/archives/best/2000/mesquite.html
https://www.gardeningknowhow.com/ornamental/trees/mesquite/mesquite-tree-uses.htm

54. Milkweed - page 101
https://milkweedbalm.com/blogs/news/not-just-a-weed-the-original-medicine-cabinet
https://www.floralencounters.com/Seeds/seed_detail.jsp?grow=Milkweed%2C+Common&productid=1242
Milkweed | The Canadian Encyclopedia
https://en.wikipedia.org/wiki/Asclepias_syriaca
Plant Details :: Milkweed (csusm.edu)
Plant Details :: Venenillo Del Rio (csusm.edu)
http://www.storey.com/article/8-native-plants-native-medicine/
Herbs, Plants, and Healing Properties – Page 7 – Legends of America
https://efotg.sc.egov.usda.gov/references/public/va/NRCS_CulturallySignificantPlants_2010.pdf
Hamel, Paul B. and Mary U. Chiltoskey, 1975 – page 44

55. Mint - page 49
23 Medicinal Plants the Native Americans Used on a Daily Basis (map-expo.com)
Herbs, Plants, and Healing Properties – Page 7 – Legends of America
https://urbansurvivalsite.com/native-american-herbs-recipes/
https://www.farmersalmanac.com/medicinal-mint-a-refreshing-remedy-18401
https://www.gardeningknowhow.com/edible/herbs/mint/how-to-grow-mint-plants-in-your-garden.htm
https://mappae.eu/herb/mint/#
Hamel, Paul B. and Mary U. Chiltoskey, 1975 - page 45

56. Mullein - page 102
https://farmhomestead.com/herbs/mullein/
Alternative Tinnitus Treatments | Arches Tinnitus Formula | Natural Treatment for Tinnitus
23 Medicinal Plants the Native Americans Used on a Daily Basis (map-expo.com)
Plant Details :: Gordolobo Muella (Edited by Diaz) (csusm.edu)
Herbs, Plants, and Healing Properties – Page 7 – Legends of America
Hamel, Paul B. and Mary U. Chiltoskey, 1975 – page 45

57. Nettle - page 103
Plant Details :: Marijuanilla (csusm.edu)
Plant Details :: Stinging nettle (csusm.edu)
Benefits Of Nettle Root – Learn How To Harvest Stinging Nettle Roots (gardeningknowhow.com)
http://www.storey.com/article/8-native-plants-native-medicine/
https://www.rjwhelan.co.nz/conditions/prostate.html

58. Oak - page 104
California live oak trees: valuable source of acorn meal for early Californians – (ethnoherbalist.com)
Plant Details :: Encino Roble (csusm.edu)
Herbs, Plants, and Healing Properties – Page 7 – Legends of America
https://www.herbazest.com/herbs/oak
https://www.rxlist.com/oak_bark/supplements.htm
Hamel, Paul B. and Mary U. Chiltoskey, 1975 – page 46

59. Oats - page 105
Plant Details :: Wild oats (csusm.edu)
Herbs, Plants, and Healing Properties – Page 7 – Legends of America
https://www.livestrong.com/article/555498-does-oatmeal-fight-cancer/
https://www.iamthegreengoddess.com/blogs/news/oatstraw

60. Oregon Grape - page 106
https://www.nps.gov/articles/000/oregon-grape.htm
https://www.stlukes-stl.com/health-content/medicine/33/000097.htm
ttps://www.oregonencyclopedia.org/articles/oregon_grape/#.Y2KR8nbP1PY
https://eflora.neocities.org/Mahonia.html

61. Osha - page 106
https://www.encyclopedia.com/medicine/drugs/pharmacology/osha
Herbs, Plants, and Healing Properties – Page 7 – Legends of America
https://nativeplants.ku.edu/ethnobotany-research/ligusticum-osha#
https://wanderingbull.com/osha-root-for-protection-energy-and-health/

62. Passionflower - page 107
Plant Details :: Passiflora (csusm.edu)
Herbs, Plants, and Healing Properties – Page 7 – Legends of America
https://www.healthyhildegard.com/passion-flower-benefits/
https://bhma.info/indications/stress-and-anxiety/passion-flower/

63. Pinon / Pinyon Pine - page 108
https://www.theforagerspath.com/educational-resources/plant-profiles/plantprofile-pinonpine/
Pinyon pine nuts, a rich source of fats and protein – (ethnoherbalist.com)
Plant Details :: Single-Leaf Pinyon Pine (csusm.edu)
http://npshistory.com/nature_notes/grca/vol8-9c.htm
Herbs, Plants, and Healing Properties – Page 7 – Legends of America
https://aromaticstudies.com/pinon-pine/
https://www.herbalremediesadvice.org/pine-properties.html

64. (White) Pine - page 108
10 Reasons You Should Be Drinking Pine Needle Tea (forestholidays.co.uk)
https://www.mayernikkitchen.com/blog/what-are-the-health-benefits-of-white-pin
Herbs, Plants, and Healing Properties – Page 9 – Legends of America
https://www.bellarmine.edu/faculty/drobinson/EasternWhitePine.asp#
https://www.mjpettengill.com/post/copy-of-the-great-white-pine-the-tree-of-peace

65. Plantain - page 109
Herbs, Plants, and Healing Properties – Page 7 – Legends of America
https://www.lrfamilydentalcare.com/blog/immediate-tooth-pain-relief-emergency-dental-care/#:~:text=Plantain
https://tonedcaribbeanbody.com/7-best-herbs-for-eye-health/
https://greenkeyhealth.co.uk/Plantain#
https://downinthewoodsltd.co.uk/native-americans-have-called-plantain-whitemans-foot/
Hamel, Paul B. and Mary U. Chiltoskey, 1975 – page 50

66. Poke Root - page 110
https://www.corinnawood.com/blog/poke-root-old-medicinal-uses
Herbs, Plants, and Healing Properties – Page 7 – Legends of America
https://www.cjmrp.com/files/the-use-of-poke-root-in-the-treatment-of-lactational-mastitis-practice-patterns-among-midwives-in-british-columbia.pdf
https://www.rjwhelan.co.nz/herbs%20A-Z/poke_root.html
Hamel, Paul B. and Mary U. Chiltoskey, 1975 – page 50

67. Prickly Pear Cactus - page 111
23 Medicinal Plants the Native Americans Used on a Daily Basis (map-expo.com)
Plant Details :: Coast Prickly Pear (csusm.edu)
Herbs, Plants, and Healing Properties – Page 7 – Legends of America
https://www.texasbeyondhistory.net/coast/nature/images/prickly-pear.html#
https://aihd.ku.edu/foods/prickly_pear_cactus.html
https://thenaturecollective.org/plant-guide/details/western-prickly-pear/
https://efotg.sc.egov.usda.gov/references/public/va/NRCS_CulturallySignificantPlants_2010.pdf

68. Rabbit Tobacco - page 111
https://gwens-nest.com/rabbit-tobacco-tincture/
https://gwens-nest.com/remedies-for-chest-congestion-rabbit-tobacco/
https://eu.tallahassee.com/story/life/home-garden/2020/12/17/one-everlastings-dont-try-puffing-rabbit-tobacco/3929610001/
Pseudognaphalium obtusifolium (blunt-leaved rabbit-tobacco): Go Botany (nativeplanttrust.org)
Home Remedies for Nasal Congestion: Rabbit Tobacco – Gwen's Nest (gwens-nest.com)
Herbs, Plants, and Healing Properties – Page 8 – Legends of America
https://tribalallianceforpollinators.com/acadp_listings/rabbit-tobacco/
https://news.emory.edu/features/2018/08/plant-hunters/index.html#group-native-american-heritage-IHwm2ri98L
Hamel, Paul B. and Mary U. Chiltoskey, 1975 – page 51

69. Red Clover - page 112
https://eu.lcsun-news.com/story/life/wellness/2016/09/01/ground-up-red-clover/87971852/
Red Clover: Benefits, Side Effects, and Preparations (verywellhealth.com)
23 Medicinal Plants the Native Americans Used on a Daily Basis (map-expo.com)
Native American Herbs May Slow Parkinson's Disease – Journal of Plant Medicines
Plant Details :: Trebolo (csusm.edu)
www.legendsofamerica.com/na-herbs/8/#R
https://www.bio-health.co.uk/red-clover-trifolium-pratense-l/
https://www.biorxiv.org/content/10.1101/2020.12.01.391268v2.full
Hamel, Paul B. and Mary U. Chiltoskey, 1975 – page 29

70. Rosemary - page 53
23 Medicinal Plants the Native Americans Used on a Daily Basis (map-expo.com)
https://urbansurvivalsite.com/native-american-herbs-recipes/
https://www.wikihow.com/Use-Rosemary-in-Cooking
https://www.gardeningknowhow.com/edible/herbs/rosemary/growing-rosemary-plants-rosemary-plant-care.htm
https://www.stylecraze.com/articles/effective-home-remedies-to-cure-jaundice/
https://www.intrepidmentalhealth.com/blog/8-ways-that-rosemary-can-improve-your-mental-emotional-and-physical-well-being#

71. Sage - page 54
https://www.healthline.com/health/sage-for-menopause
23 Medicinal Plants the Native Americans Used on a Daily Basis (map-expo.com)
White sage (Salvia apiana): an important ceremonial and medicinal plant for Native Americans – (ethnoherbalist.com)
Plant Details :: White sage (csusm.edu)
Plant Details :: Salvia apiana Jeps. (csusm.edu)
https://www.ictinc.ca/blog/aboriginal-sacred-plants-sage
Herbs, Plants, and Healing Properties – Page 8 – Legends of America
https://www.breastfeedingbasics.com/articles/lactation-suppression#:~:text=Sage

72. Saltbush - page 113
Four wing saltbush plant, seeds for food and leaves for lather. – (ethnoherbalist.com)
Herbs, Plants, and Healing Properties – Page 8 – Legends of America
https://issuu.com/westernaglife/docs/westernaglifemagazine_summer2019_si/s/112412
https://www.fs.usda.gov/wildflowers/plant-of-the-week/atriplex_canescens.shtml#

73. Sarsaparilla - page 114
Sarsaparilla: The Benefits, Risks, and Side Effects (healthline.com)
https://www.spiceography.com/sarsaparilla/
Sarsaparilla (ku.edu)
Sarsaparilla: Health Benefits, Side Effects, Uses, Dose & Precautions (rxlist.com)
Herbs, Plants, and Healing Properties – Page 8 – Legends of America
https://www.carahealth.com/herbal-monographs/sarsaparilla-smilax-ornata
https://www.indigo-herbs.co.uk/natural-health-guide/benefits/sarsaparilla#

74. Sassafras - page 115
Herbs, Plants, and Healing Properties – Page 8 – Legends of America
https://www.healthbenefitstimes.com/sassafras/
https://www.rxlist.com/sassafras/supplements.htm#
https://www.webmd.com/vitamins/ai/ingredientmono-674/sassafras
https://efotg.sc.egov.usda.gov/references/public/va/NRCS_CulturallySignificantPlants_2010.pdf
Hamel, Paul B. and Mary U. Chiltoskey, 1975 – page 54

75. Saw Palmetto - page 115
https://justglowingwithhealth.com/guest-posthow-to-brew-saw-palmetto-herbal-tea/
https://www.healthline.com/nutrition/saw-palmetto#what-it-is
23 Medicinal Plants the Native Americans Used on a Daily Basis (map-expo.com)
Inflammation and Native American medicine: the role of botanicals | The American Journal of Clinical Nutrition | Oxford Academic (oup.com)
Saw Palmetto | British Herbal Medicine Association (bhma.info)
https://www.healthline.com/nutrition/saw-palmetto
Herbs, Plants, and Healing Properties – Page 8 – Legends of America
https://www.healthline.com/nutrition/saw-palmetto-benefits#5.-May-help-regulate-testosterone-levels

76. Seneca Snakeroot - page 116
http://medicinalherbinfo.org/000Herbs2016/1herbs/senega-snakeroot/
https://www.botanical.com/botanical/mgmh/s/senega41.html
https://pfaf.org/user/Plant.aspx?LatinName=Polygala+senega
https://www.drugs.com/npp/senega-root.html
https://www.pioneerbushcraft.org/nature-articles/bushcraft-articles/heath-milkwort-snakes/
https://www.thefreelibrary.com/Seneca+snakeroot%3A+an+important+medicinal+plant.+(Gardening+In...-a094078494
Hamel, Paul B. and Mary U. Chiltoskey, 1975 – page 55

77. Skullcap - page 117
Skullcap: The Nerve Soothing Herb | The Alchemist's Kitchen (thealchemistskitchen.com)
Skullcap: Potential Medicinal Crop (purdue.edu)
Herbs, Plants, and Healing Properties – Page 8 – Legends of America
https://www.mountsinai.org/health-library/herb/skullcap#
https://www.webmd.com/vitamins/ai/ingredientmono-986/skullcap
https://www.indigo-herbs.co.uk/natural-health-guide/benefits/skullcap
Hamel, Paul B. and Mary U. Chiltoskey, 1975 – page 55

78. Slippery Elm - page 118
https://www.mountsinai.org/health-library/herb/slippery-elm
23 Medicinal Plants the Native Americans Used on a Daily Basis (map-expo.com)
Herbs, Plants, and Healing Properties – Page 8 – Legends of America
https://facty.com/food/nutrition/surprising-health-benefits-of-slippery-elm/4/
https://www.medicalnewstoday.com/articles/slippery-elm
https://www.indigo-herbs.co.uk/natural-health-guide/benefits/slippery-elm-bark
Hamel, Paul B. and Mary U. Chiltoskey, 1975 – page 33

79. St. John's Wort - page 118
Inflammation and Native American medicine: the role of botanicals | The American Journal of Clinical Nutrition | Oxford Academic (oup.com)
St. John's wort for depression (ethnoherbalist.com)
Herbs, Plants, and Healing Properties – Page 8 – Legends of America
https://www.healthline.com/health/shingles-natural-treatment#6.-Homeopathic-or-herbal-remedies
https://www.nccih.nih.gov/health/st-johns-wort#
https://www.webmd.com/vitamins/ai/ingredientmono-329/st-johns-wort
https://www.bocaratonfootcare.com/herbal-aids-for-varicose-veins/#

80. Stoneseed - page 119
https://pfaf.org/user/Plant.aspx?LatinName=Lithospermum+ruderale
https://www.planetayurveda.com/western-stoneseed-lithospermum-ruderale/
Herbs, Plants, and Healing Properties – Page 8 – Legends of America
https://keys2liberty.wordpress.com/tag/stoneseed/
https://www.nps.gov/brca/learn/nature/showystoneseed.htm

81. Sumac - page 57
23 Medicinal Plants the Native Americans Used on a Daily Basis (map-expo.com)
Herbs, Plants, and Healing Properties – Page 8 – Legends of America
https://urbansurvivalsite.com/native-american-herbs-recipes/
https://www.doityourself.com/stry/10-shrubs-for-beautiful-fall-color
https://www.masterclass.com/articles/what-is-sumac-learn-how-to-use-sumac-with-tips-and-8-sumac-recipes
https://www.sawmillherbfarm.com/herb%20profile/staghorn-sumac/#:~:text=Sumac
Hamel, Paul B. and Mary U. Chiltoskey, 1975 – page 57

82. Sweetgrass - page 120
Sweetgrass | The Canadian Encyclopedia
Herbs, Plants, and Healing Properties – Page 8 – Legends of America
https://www.nrcs.usda.gov/plant-materials/news/sweetgrass
http://www.nativetech.org/plants/sweetgrass.html

83. Thyme / Wild Mountain Thyme - page 121
https://www.herbalgram.org/resources/herbalgram/issues/80/table-of-contents/article3352/
https://www.medicalnewstoday.com/articles/266016
http://medicinalherbinfo.org/000Herbs2016/1herbs/thyme/
https://map-expo.com/highlights/23-medicinal-plants-native-americans-used-daily-basis/

84. Tobacco - page 122
https://www.ncbi.nlm.nih.gov/pmc/articles/PMC1079499/
Plant Details :: Desert Tabacco (csusm.edu)

Herbs, Plants, and Healing Properties – Page 9 – Legends of America
https://keepitsacred.itcmi.org/tobacco-and-tradition/traditional-tobacco-use/
Traditional Tobacco and American Indian Communities in Minnesota - Commercial Tobacco Prevention and Control
https://www.utep.edu/herbal-safety/herbal-facts/herbal%20facts%20sheet/tobacco.html#
Hamel, Paul B. and Mary U. Chiltoskey, 1975 – page 59

85. Uva Ursi - page 122
https://www.healthguideinfo.com/herbal-medicine/p91393/
23 Medicinal Plants the Native Americans Used on a Daily Basis (map-expo.com)
Plant Details :: Coralillo (csusm.edu)
Plant Details :: Manzanita (csusm.edu)
Herbs, Plants, and Healing Properties – Page 9 – Legends of America
https://newrootsherbal.com/product/id/0820
Hamel, Paul B. and Mary U. Chiltoskey, 1975 – page 25

86. Valerian - page 123
Plant Details :: Valeriana (csusm.edu)
https://theherbalacademy.com/getting-to-know-the-valerian-plant/
Herbs, Plants, and Healing Properties – Page 9 – Legends of America
https://www.nativeamericantea.com/taste-of-tradition-blog/chamomile-and-valerian-root-together/

87. Western Skunk Cabbage - page 124
https://www.legendsofamerica.com/na-herbs/9/#W
https://www.oregonencyclopedia.org/articles/skunk-cabbage/#.Y0Bgc3bMJPY
https://www.fs.usda.gov/wildflowers/plant-of-the-week/Lysichiton-americanus.shtml
https://colombia.inaturalist.org/posts/69847-western-skunk-cabbage-journal-9-9-22

88. White Willow - page 125
https://joybileefarm.com/willow-bark-for-herbal-remedies/
http://www.storey.com/article/8-native-plants-native-medicine/
https://www.mountsinai.org/health-library/herb/willow-bark#
https://www.brenhamfamilydental.com/four-home-remedies-to-help-you-with-the-pain-of-dental-infection.php#
Hamel, Paul B. and Mary U. Chiltoskey, 1975 – page 61

89. Wild Black Cherry - page 126
Herbs, Plants, and Healing Properties – Page 9 – Legends of America
https://www.webmd.com/vitamins/ai/ingredientmono-888/wild-cherry#
https://www.indigo-herbs.co.uk/natural-health-guide/benefits/wild-cherry
https://www.eclecticschoolofherbalmedicine.com/wild-cherry/
Hamel, Paul B. and Mary U. Chiltoskey, 1975 – pages 28/29

90. Wild Carrot - page 127
https://www.rxlist.com/wild_carrot/supplements.htm
https://www.survivalsullivan.com/wild-carrots-queen-anns-lace/
https://www.legendsofamerica.com/na-herbs/9/#W
https://www.eattheweeds.com/daucus-carota-pusillus-edible-wild-carrots-2/

91. Wild Ginger - page 128
23 Medicinal Plants the Native Americans Used on a Daily Basis (map-expo.com)
https://www.wildflower.org/plants/result.php?id_plant=asca

https://www.fs.usda.gov/wildflowers/plant-of-the-week/asarum_canadense.shtml
https://specialtyproduce.com/produce/Wild_Ginger_Roots_12187.php
Herbs, Plants, and Healing Properties – Page 9 – Legends of America
https://efotg.sc.egov.usda.gov/references/public/va/NRCS_CulturallySignificantPlants_2010.pdf
https://medicinalgardens.web.unc.edu/wild-ginger/
https://www.ncbi.nlm.nih.gov/pmc/articles/PMC4818021/
Hamel, Paul B. and Mary U. Chiltoskey, 1975 – page 36

92. Wild Lettuce - page 128
https://www.legendsofamerica.com/na-herbs/9/#W
https://www.webmd.com/vitamins/ai/ingredientmono-342/wild-lettuce#
https://www.verywellhealth.com/the-benefits-of-wild-lettuce-88661
https://www.indigo-herbs.co.uk/natural-health-guide/benefits/wild-lettuce
https://www.healthline.com/nutrition/wild-lettuce

93. Wild Rose / hips - page 129
23 Medicinal Plants the Native Americans Used on a Daily Basis (map-expo.com)
Wild rose hips, an attractive source of vitamins for Native Americans – (ethnoherbalist.com)
Plant Details :: California wild rose (csusm.edu)
Plant Details :: Rosa de Castilla (csusm.edu)
Herbs, Plants, and Healing Properties – Page 9 – Legends of America
https://naturescalendar.woodlandtrust.org.uk/blog/2021/dog-rose-meaning-myth-and-medicinal-uses/

94. Wild Yam - page 130
https://the-natural-web.org/2014/01/11/wild-yam/
Herbs, Plants, and Healing Properties – Page 9 – Legends of America
https://www.rxlist.com/wild_yam/supplements.htm#
https://www.motherearthliving.com/gardening/herb-to-know-wild-yam/
https://mountainx.com/living/farm-garden/wild_things_indigenous_wild_yam/

95. Witch Hazel - page 131
https://www.legendsofamerica.com/na-herbs/9/#W
https://www.haverford.edu/arboretum/blog/wonders-witch-hazel#
https://www.theatlantic.com/health/archive/2012/11/the-mysterious-past-and-present-of-witch-hazel/264553/
https://www.almanac.com/witch-hazel-native-shrub-worth-knowing
Hamel, Paul B. and Mary U. Chiltoskey, 1975 – page 62

96. Wormwood - page 132
http://www.naturalmedicinalherbs.net/herbs/a/artemisia-campestris=field-southernwood.php
Plant Details :: Worm Wood (csusm.edu)
https://www.legendsofamerica.com/na-herbs/9/#W
https://www.stlukes-stl.com/health-content/medicine/33/000097.htm

97. Yarrow - page 59
How to Grow and Care for Yarrow | Gardener's Path (gardenerspath.com)
23 Medicinal Plants the Native Americans Used on a Daily Basis (map-expo.com)
Plant Details :: yarrow (csusm.edu)
https://www.eatweeds.co.uk/yarrow-achillea-millefolium
Herbs, Plants, and Healing Properties – Page 9 – Legends of America
https://urbansurvivalsite.com/native-american-herbs-recipes/

https://www.gardeningknowhow.com/edible/herbs/yarrow/growing-yarrow.htm
https://www.bionity.com/en/encyclopedia/Achillea_millefolium.html
https://www.drugs.com/npc/yarrow.html#:~:text=Yarrow
Hamel, Paul B. and Mary U. Chiltoskey, 1975 – page 62

98. Yellow Dock - page 132
https://www.legendsofamerica.com/na-herbs/9/#W
https://www.webmd.com/vitamins/ai/ingredientmono-651/yellow-dock
https://healthyeating.sfgate.com/health-benefits-yellow-dock-tea-10536.html
https://seedsandplants.co.za/herbal-remedies/yellow-dock-medicinal-uses/
Hamel, Paul B. and Mary U. Chiltoskey, 1975 – page 32

99. Yerba Santa / Mountain Balm - page 133
https://www.rxlist.com/yerba_santa/supplements.htm
Traditional yerba santa uses: the sacred herb – (ethnoherbalist.com)
Plant Details :: Yerba santa (csusm.edu)
https://www.legendsofamerica.com/na-herbs/9/#W
https://www.salk.edu/news-release/native-california-medicinal-plant-may-hold-promise-for-treating-alzheimers/#

100. Yew - page 134
https://www.wascocountylibrary.com/pacific-northwest-plant-of-the-day/2020/4/22/pacific-northwest-plant-of-the-day-pacific-yew
http://www.storey.com/article/8-native-plants-native-medicine/
https://www.bellarmine.edu/faculty/drobinson/yew.htm#
http://www.native-languages.org/legends-yew.htm

101.Yucca - page 135
Banana yucca, a source of soap and seed flour for desert settlers – (ethnoherbalist.com)
Plant Details :: Chaparral Yucca (csusm.edu)
YUCCA: Overview, Uses, Side Effects, Precautions, Interactions, Dosing and Reviews (webmd.com)
https://www.nps.gov/band/learn/historyculture/native-plant-use.htm#:~:text=Yucca

BOOKS AND BACKGROUND READING

Hamel, Paul B. and Mary U. Chiltoskey, 1975,
Cherokee Plants and Their Uses – A 400 Year History, N.C. Herald Publishing Co.

Weiner, Michael A., 1991,
Earth Medicine-Earth Food: Plant Remedies, Drugs, and Natural Foods of the North American Indians,
Fawcett Books.

Garrett, JT and Garrett, Michael, 1996,
Medicine of the Cherokee: The Way of Right Relationship,
Bear & Company.

Tilford, Gregory, 1997,
Edible and Medicinal Plants of the West,
Mountain Press.

Karalliedde, Dr. L., and Gawaarammana, Dr. I., 2007,
Traditional Herbal Medicines, A Guide to their Safer Use,
Hammersmith Press Ltd.

National Library of Medicine. (n.d.). Medicine Ways: Traditional Healers and Healing. [Blog post]. Retrieved from https://www.nlm.nih.gov/nativevoices/exhibition/healing-ways/medicine-ways/healing-plants.html

North American Native Plant Society. (n.d.). Plant database. [Online database]. NANPS
Cherokee Agriculture – Blue Ridge National Heritage Area (blueridgeheritage.com)
Moore, Michael, 1979, *Medicinal Plants of the Mountain West,* Museum of New Mexico Press.

Moore, Michael, 1994,
Specific Indications for Herbs in General Use, Southwest School of Herbal Medicine, 1994.
http://swsbm.henriettesherbal.com/ManualsMM/SpecIndic3.pdf

Moore, Michael, 1995, 'Herbal Materia Medica', Southwest School of Herbal Medicine.
https://pdf4pro.com/view/herbal-materia-medica-michael-moore-4942.html

Moore, Michael, 1995, 'Herb/Medicine Contraindications', Southwest School of Herbal Medicine.
http://www.losolivos-obgyn.com/info/nutrition/HerbMedContra.pdf

J.L. Longe, editor, 'The Gale Encyclopedia of Alternative Medicine', 2nd Edition (2005).

Hull, K. (MD) and Hull, M. (MD), 2010,
Indiana Medical History Museum Guide to the Medicinal Plant Garden.
https://www.imhm.org/resources/Documents/Binder1_MPG_Guide_2010_sfs.pdf

Reid, S., Wishingrad, V., and McCabe, Stephen, 2009,
Native American Uses of California Plants – Ethnobotany,
University of California, Santa Cruz Arboretum.
https://arboretum.ucsc.edu/pdfs/ethnobotany-webversion.pdf

PICTURE REFERENCES

Photographs inside this book were purchased from Depositphotos: https://depositphotos.com/home.html
under license https://depositphotos.com/license.html
Each photograph number ID and contributor is listed. Exceptions from other sources are listed.

Front cover - Depositphotos 255633104 @ NatashaBreen
Inside cover - 86907244 @ Cornfield
Title page - photo by Chanhee Lee on Unsplash
https://unsplash.com/photos/person-in-black-jacket-holding-white-powder-VzevMkifEMw

Opposite copyright page - photo by Logan Mayer on Unsplash - https://unsplash.com/photos/ZgTwCfKIyNQ
About the author - photo by Rasa Kasparaviciene on Unsplash - https://unsplash.com/photos/5AZMvtjCbd4
Opposite contents page - photo by Annie Spratt on Unsplash - https://unsplash.com/photos/4IqTki_q8KI
Page 1 'Part one - Jacob's Story' 255220184 @.shock
Page 2 - Photo by Anshu A on Unsplash - https://unsplash.com/photos/Iokj6jEwkxM
Pages 6/7 - 204092874 @ ChamilleWhite
Pages 8/9 - 362353537 @ xhico

Page 10 - photo by Artem Shuba on Unsplash - https://unsplash.com/photos/NKopLg8YrO8
Page 13 – 10324766 @ PiLens
Page 15 - 11420771 @Enigmangels
Pages 16/17 - photo by Andrew James on Unsplash - https://unsplash.com/photos/ehdsg7SHm6A
Page 19 - 5992439 @ billperry
Page 20 - 556677044 @ shutterbug68
Page 21 - 425117248 @ nailotl
Page 21 - 432958694 @ iker.zabaleta
Page 22 - 9619338 @ Klanneke
Page 24/25 - 293247148 @ j.chizhe
Page 26 - photo by Zuzana Kacerová on Unsplash - https://unsplash.com/de/fotos/fOKx5IOniXk
Page 31 - 143959477 @ JanPietruszka
Page 32/33 - 47145049 @ sauletas
Page 34 - photo by Annie Spratt on Unsplash https://unsplash.com/photos/vuC7P3tUA20
Page 36 - Blackberry - 86238866 @ Valentyn_Volkov
Page 39 - Buckbrush - 318642974 @ ovju
Page 40 - Cattails - 391523920 @ Fahroni
Page 42 - Dandelions - 370362384 @ MadeleineSteinbach
Page 44 - Elderflower - 73641729 @ re_bekka
Page 45 - Elderberries - 396061674 @ HJBC
Page 47 - Flaxseed - 46405899 @ HappyCity
Page 49 - Mint 397954516 @ teine26
Page 50/51 - 269257946 @ robertprzybysz
Page 53 - Rosemary - 48477813 @ scis65
Page 55 - Sage - 354154492 @ antmos
Page 56 - Sage - 32692027 @ yulan
Page 57 - Sumac - 298719466 @ weha
Page 58 - Sumac dried - 183125492 @ lvenks
Page 59 - Yarrow white- 242655006 @ Hannah1982
Page 60 - Yarrow red -295633104 @ ovju
Page 62/63 - 194209222 @ Nikolay_Donetsk
Page 66 - 363437456 @ Nastyaofly
Page 67 - Aloe vera - 293871106 @ areeya
Page 68 - Angelica - 370067802 @ woff1966
Page 69 - Arnica - 268524186 @ daniilphotos
Page 70 - Black cohosh - 477391976 ovju
Page 70 - Black haw -446405360 @ sstandbridge
Page 71 - Blue cohosh - photograph by Eric Hunt. https://commons.wikimedia.org/w/index.php?curid=84068191
Link to license: https://creativecommons.org/licenses/by/4.0/
Page 72 - Boneset - 542798070 @ ChWeiss
Page 72 - Borage - 182256564 @ coramueller
Page 73 - Boswellia - 185619324 @ jochenschneider
Page 74 - Broom snakeweed 430668878 @ Twoscorpions
Page 75 - Buffaloberry 340342586 @ PantherMediaSeller
Page 75 - Burdock 144731801 @ 13-Smile
Page 76 - California poppy 478009098 @ mschuppi
Page 77 - Cat's claw 228936290 @ jcsmilly
Page 78 - Cedar - 176246458 @ wrangel
Page 78 - Centaury - 55058639 @ Lumitar
Page 79 - Chamomile - 316946838 @ orestligetka

Page 80 - Chasteberry - 464122890 @ RUPENDRA143
Page 80 - Chickweed - 75449569 @ tverkhovinets
Page 81 - Chokeberry - 50511323 @ voljurij
Page 82 - Cleavers - 150859112 @ christening
Page 82 - Coltsfoot - 109812530 @ 13-Smile
Page 83 - Comfrey - 65993523 @ vladvitek
Page 83 - Damiana - 332158450 @ kip02kas
Page 84 - Devil's claw - 318831742 @ nahhan
Page 85 - Dogwood - 34578287 @ kathyclark
Page 86 - Echinacea - 283976664 @ weha
Page 86 - Evening primrose - 402261400 @ Tarkus
Page 87 - American feverfew - photograph by Peter Chen
https://en.wikipedia.org/wiki/File:Parthenium_integrifolium-flowering.jpg
Link to license: https://en.wikipedia.org/wiki/en:Creative_Commons
Page 88 / Feverfew - 78875616 @ HeikeRau
Page 88 - Feverwort - purchased from Shutterstock 1312141907 (photo by K Hanley CHDPhoto)
Link to license: Shutterstock Standard License
Page 89 - Garlic - 540575012 @ OlesySH
Page 89 - Wild Garlic - 154401606 @ pellegrino13
Page 90 - Gentiana - 129475478 @ digidream
Page 90 - American ginseng - 375528014 @ KatiesPostcard
Page 91 - Goldenrod - 322341960 @ ekina1
Page 92 - Goldenseal plant - 489238058 @ meunierd
Page 92 - Goldenseal root - 104751078 @ marilyna
Page 93 - Gravel root - 508348254 @ Debu55y
Page 93 - Hawthorn - 61332609 @ tarasylo
Page 94 - Western hemlock - 404869642 @ HanjoHellmann
Page 94 - Eastern hemlock - 98249986 @ Wirepec
Page 95 - Honeysuckle - 5347851 @ shiyali
Page 96 - Hops - 83779584 @ alaindemaximy
Page 97 - Horsemint - 77667842 @ anothervue
Page 97 - Horsetail - 153484028 @ coramueller
Page 98 - Juniper - 56237111 @ oksixx
Page 99 - Desert lavender - Desert Lavender photograph by Stan Shebs.
https://en.m.wikipedia.org/wiki/File:Hyptis_emoryi.jpg
Link to license: https://creativecommons.org/licenses/by-sa/3.0/deed.en
Page 100 - Lemon balm - 11218088 @ Aviavlad3
Page 101 - Mesquite - 393932590 @ Twoscorpions
Page 101 - Milkweed - 75463281 @ alaindemaximy
Page 102 - Mullein - 100685146 @ ingridhs
Page 103 - Nettle - 34049521 @ Cosmin35
Page 104 - Oak - 313997584 @ fermate
Page 105 - Oats 1 - 4730513 @ Tamara_k
Page 105 - Oats 2 - 323712896 @ YAYImages
Page 106 – Oregon grape - 378444670 @ BestPhotoStudio
Page 106 - Osha flower 79718106 @ teresinagoia
Page 106 - Osha root - 323170134 @ spline_x
Page 107 - Passionflower - 63374315 @ scis65
Page 108 - Pinyon pine - 211090112 @ AnalacobPhotography
Page 108 - White pine - 158788020 @ aleksander

Page 109 - Plantain - 347788717 @ ChamilleWhite
Page 110 - Poke root - 170160306 @ MIMOHE
Page 111 - Prickly pear cactus - 311504618 @ gpiazzese
Page 111 - Rabbit tobacco - photograph by Sheila Collins Bourgoin. https://inaturalist.ala.org.au/observations/31527846
Link to license: https://creativecommons.org/licenses/by/4.0/
Page 112 - Red clover - 380566966 @ stefans42
Page 113 - Saltbush - purchased from Shutterstock 1869510838 (photo by Jared Quentin)
Link to license: Standard Shutterstock License
Page 114 - Sarsaparilla dried – 163135020 @ Luisecheverriurrea
Page 115 - Sassafras – 515955568 @ befehr
Page 115 - Saw palmetto plant – 9938986 @ Wirepec
Page 115 - Saw palmetto berries – 10531215 @ Quasarphoto
Page 116 - Seneca snakeroot plant – purchased from Shutterstock 2224961039 (photo by Sabar Widodo)
Link to license: Standard Shutterstock License
Page 116 - Seneca snakeroot dried – 6304075 @ marilyna
Page 117 - Skullcap – 7624577 @ MonaMakela
Page 118 - Slippery elm – 306789600 @ narcoz52
Page 118 - St John's Wort – 251391292 @ ChamilleWhite
Page 119 - Stoneseed – purchased from iStock (photo by Gerald Corsi) Stock file ID 1406377363
Link to license: https://www.istockphoto.com/legal/license-agreement
Page 120 - Sweetgrass – 116286146 @ oleghz
Page 121 - Thyme – 11225138 @ fisfra
Page 121 - Wild Mountain thyme – 35436499 @ Mirage3
Page 122 - Tobacco – 139999502 @ stoonn
Page 122 - Uva ursi – 268865376 @ cadama
Page 123 - Valerian plant – 333064412 @ martiroz
Page 123 - Valerian flower – 407710114 @ Anastasiia.Malinich
Page 124 - Western skunk cabbage – 205012686 @ manfredxy
Page 125 - White willow tree – 451688680 @ Wirestock
Page 125 - Willow bark – 37603919 @ Kalcutta
Page 126 - Wild black cherry plant - 514174294 @ weha
Page 126 - Wild black cherries – 6899397 @ O.Rohulya
Page 127 - Wild carrot – 79821748 @ chungking
Page 128 - Wild ginger – 582455032 @ anmbph
Page 128 - Wild lettuce – purchased from iStock (photo by Kamila Koziot) Stock file ID 1403254847
Link to license: https://www.istockphoto.com/legal/license-agreement
Page 129 - Wild rose flower – purchased from Shutterstock 1572214741 (photo by off the beaten path)
https://www.shutterstock.com/image-photo/close-pink-wild-rose-flofer-rosa-1572214741
Link to license: Shutterstock Standard License
Page 129 - Rosehips purchased from Shutterstock 2035998926
(photo by Nataliia Suietska) https://www.shutterstock.com/image-photo/large-rose-hips-rosa-acicularis-bush-2035998926
Link to license: Shutterstock Standard License
Page 130 - Wild yam purchased from iStock (photo by chengyuzheng) Stock file Id 134725390
Link to license: https://www.istockphoto.com/legal/license-agreement
Page 131 - Witch hazel – 179731482 @ EBFoto
Page 132 - Wormwood – 346373552 @ orestligetka
Page 132 - Yellow dock plant - 403242236 @ arousa
Page 132 - Yellow dock root – 23145296 @ czuber
Page 133 - Yerba santa plant – 417727738 @ Twoscorpions
Page 133 - Yerba santa leaves – 172745920 @ marilyna

Page 134 - Yew – 540646746 @ annaleb06
Page 135 - Yucca – 137484910 @ kamchatka
Page 136/7 - 257389782 @ robertprzybysz
Page 150/1 - 52081547 @ JanPietruszka
Page 158/9 - 50374237 @ ChamilleWhite
Page 160 - photo by Antonio Cogo on Unsplash https://unsplash.com/photos/BvyRYcZgVsI
Page 163 - photo by Madison Podjasek on Unsplash https://unsplash.com/photos/rul8f2bcoFs
Page 186/7 - 275673152 @ ChamilleWhite

Made in the USA
Columbia, SC
21 July 2024

8284daf0-f2dd-411b-912d-94dc6c996cbdR01